SURVIVING ALCOHOLIC PARENTS

A TEEN'S ABC GUIDE TO THRIVING IN A WORLD OF CHAOS

Written By

Tammy Vincent

Summary: A self-help guide for teenagers with alcoholic parents. Discusses tips, tricks and methods to help cope with current situations. Provides resources and links to go for support.

ISBN: 979-8-218-09880-3

WHAT OTHERS ARE SAYING ABOUT TAMMY VINCENT AND HER STRATEGIES

"Wow. The chapter on empathy was so so moving. How we can better understand people to be able to help them? We can be so grateful in the treasure, called Tammy, to be so courageous & transparent in sharing her journey with us. " - Damita C.

 Whitener user

★★★★★ **For those who can relate, absolutely get this!**
Reviewed in the United States on November 2, 2022

I loved everything about this! If you know of anyone dealing with this kind of situation, by all means, I highly recommend this book. Just going through the motions and the challenging things one has to endure, this book teaches the individual how to move on regardless. It was an amazing read!

"Tammy, you are able to truly engage your reader. Once engaged, the honesty you deliver allows that child a space of self-forgiveness and permission to be released from guilt. Powerful and Moving." - Dr. Vedell

★★★★★ **A Must Have for Resource Libraries!**
Reviewed in the United States on October 18, 2022
Verified Purchase

As an online course creator and empowerment coach, this is the type of resource I'd recommend to my clients and students. This author brilliantly, yet simplistically provides much needed information, insight, and practical strategies to overcome trauma & stigma associated with addiction of loved ones. I'm definitely adding the paperback to my list of library resources!

"Self-care and strength to survive comes exploding through. Like Yoda, Tammy delivers words of wisdom and courage." Jill Weiland, a forever grateful student

THE IDEAL SPEAKER FOR YOUR NEXT EVENT!

If you're ready to help empower the young adults you know by showing them safe ways to identify problems, learn self-love strategies, conquer misguided perceptions of alcoholism, and thrive against the damaging effects of alcoholism in the home, you will love having Tammy Vincent as your next guest speaker!

To Inquire About Bookings Contact:

Tammy Vincent

513-280-3555

teensthrivingnow@gmail.com

DEDICATION:

This book is dedicated to my three children (Dakota, Jessica and Derek) and my husband, Greg, who love me for who I am; my friends for sticking with me through my journey, and all my friends at Al-anon and ACOA who over the years showed me there was a way to find true happiness. And lastly, to my late parents, who throughout all their struggles, loved me the best way they knew how.

I would also like to acknowledge David and Jason Benham, who during a listening prayer at a 2021 conference spoke to me and told me it was time; to James Malinchak for the encouragement and to Nick and Megan Unsworth who supplied me with the tools to get it done.

SURVIVING ALCOHOLIC PARENTS:

A Teens ABC Guide to Thriving In A World Of Chaos

TABLE OF CONTENTS:

A MESSAGE TO YOU

Growing up the child of an alcoholic is the ultimate test of strength, courage, resilience and character. Unfortunately, many children are tested way before they are emotionally and mentally equipped to deal with this level of dysfunction. Their days are filled with fear and anxiety. They are witness to and part of atrocities that nobody on this earth should have to endure, especially not children. They are left to their own devices to do anything they can to just get to the next day. More days than not, they are hyper-focused on doing nothing more than just surviving.

I know all this, not because I read books, watched movies, or became a child psychiatrist, but simply because I lived it, and ultimately survived it.

Both of my parents were alcoholics from as early as I can remember. My mother was a more stereotypical drunk; violent, abusive, mean and embarrassing to be around more often than not.

My father, whom I loved dearly, was what I would have considered a "functional alcoholic". While I never had to endure the pain from him physically, and he rarely even raised his voice to us kids, we still took the brunt of his addiction into our adult years, and there were still battle wounds we all acquired, nonetheless. My older brother, myself and my younger sister all lived in the same house with the same parents. We experienced the same dysfunction, the same confusion, and the same instability of family life. It is amazing, then, that we all reacted so differently to our environment. We developed our own coping skills and drew our own conclusions and perceptions of the events that unfolded on a daily basis. It was as if we did not even grow up in the same household. However, the one thing we all had in common was the unspoken rule of a house with an addict among it. The family motto "Don't talk, don't feel, don't trust" was taken to heart, and we never told a soul. We didn't even talk about it among ourselves until well into our adulthood.

However, now, after years of help and research, it is time to talk.

This time, however, I want to talk to you, and anybody else that is suffering from the effects of an alcoholic parent. If you are reading this book, I am going to assume one of two things... Either you are the child of an alcoholic, or you know and care about someone who is and you want to see if this book is for them. Am I correct?

Well, you are not alone. Right now there are over 18 million children suffering the effects of living with an addicted parent. That is nearly one in four, the majority of them being alcoholics. To me that number seems staggering. Eighteen million confused, lonely, scared, and abused innocent children who don't know where to turn for help. Many of them don't even know there are options. Well, I am here to help. I have made it my personal mission to eradicate the damaging effects of alcoholic parents for children across the globe. And I will not stop until I am done.

When you have time, go to Google or get on your phone and type in Children of Alcoholics. What comes up? "Welcome-Adult Children of Alcoholics" That is what comes up on my phone. So it got me thinking....

Why can't I do more to reach the CHILDREN of ALCOHO-LICS before they are adults? That is when they need us. That is when they are hurting, confused and lost. That is when they are developing lifelong coping skills and habits based off of a completely dysfunctional situation. What if I could teach them and equip them with tools and resources to help them through these difficult times? What if I could show them that no matter how hard it gets, that self care is the answer? Why should we wait until the damage is done and they are adults? Let's get started now!

This is now my personal mission. To eradicate the damaging effects of alcoholic parents across the country. To provide resources and education so that they can have a chance at what some children would consider a normal life. To make them understand that throughout this entire process, no matter how hard it is to believe right now, that there is nothing more important than taking care of YOU! My prayer for the outcome of this book is to just lead children to understand that there is help out there, that their only job is to love and take care of themselves, and that there is help all along the way.

I am not saying I am a doctor, therapist, or counselor. What I am saying is that I've been working on healing from my own personal trauma of not one, but two alcoholic parents. I have learned a lot along the way. Thousands of hours of reading, workshops, practice, and Al-anon meetings have gone a long way towards my healing. I am still on that journey, and always will be. It's the journey of a lifetime. And now I want to invite you to start your own personal healing journey, knowing that there are people beside you every step of the way.

They say that alcoholism is a family disease and that could not be any further from the truth. Absolutely nobody escapes the backlash of what happens when there is an active alcoholic in the house. There are so many different feelings of guilt, anger, shame, rage, terror, and love all mixed together. The family dynamic and people's roles in the family changes constantly. Children are neglected and left to tend to themselves. Codependency occurs, and in the end, if left untreated, everyone in the family turns into the alcoholic, whether or not they ever take a drink.

However, if we are aware of these dynamics, we can adapt and make the situation bearable. We can learn what to do and what not to do, and why we are doing it. We can learn how to cope with the alcoholic while also learning how to maintain our own sense of self and sanity. We can thrive during this time, by learning just a few simple tips and tricks that I have included in the book.

Ultimately, we can learn to take care of ourselves.

I am not going to say this is going to be an easy journey.

There will be hardship and heartache. There will be pain and suffering. Bad things will happen. There is nothing you can do about it and nothing I can do to stop it either. Fortunately, with work and understanding, you can remain strong throughout this journey. You can become the "You" you were meant to be. God put you on this Earth to do amazing things. He put you here to be a victor, not a victim. He gave ME the strength to get through this so that I could be a voice of strength for you, and point you in the direction of happiness. I urge you to take what you like from here, leave the rest, and start on your journey to be a THRIVER, not just a survivor.

ACCEPTANCE

"The First Part Of Transformation is Awareness. The second part is Acceptance"[i]

The words acceptance, admission, awareness and acknowledgement are all terms that can be interchanged in this book, but the meaning remains the same for all of them. You have concluded, without a doubt, that an alcoholic in your life is spinning your life out of control. You realize that your life is far from what would be considered NORMAL, and you are longing to do something about it. Well, that is what we are here to do. Not to blow smoke up your butt and tell you that at the snap of a finger, and the reading of this book, that your life will go from your own private hell that you are living into a life full of serenity and bliss. No, that would be a lie. However, what I can tell you is that you are at the right place; and with a lot of work, an open mind, and an honest desire to be the best you can be in a world throwing nothing but crap at you right now, you can get closer to the life you desire. And even more exciting is knowing you do not have to wait until the effects of living with an alcoholic have destroyed you… You can start to heal right now, BEFORE the damage is done. The fact that you have accepted that there is a problem that needs to be worked on is the first step in the right direction. Congratulations.

For the purpose of simplicity and knowing that the alcoholic in your family can be a male or female, we will just call this person your alcoholic. This is the person whose drinking has caused your situation to become what it is, and the cause of you being here reading this book in the first place.

Do you even remember the moment that you accepted that your life was out of your control due to someone else's drinking? That your family life was far from peaceful, happy or even content. It may have been a single incident but most likely it was not. Most likely it was subtle constant events that made you realize things were just not right. You may have helped your father or mother fix their drinks from the time you could barely walk. You may have covered up your alcoholic when they fell asleep on the couch every weekend for months. You may have even held their hair back while they vomited, or picked them up from jail for wrecking the family car. Whatever the situation is, the fact that you accepted that changes must be made for the sake of your own sanity is the very first step towards recovery.

For me the moment was instantaneous, and the shame and embarrassment I felt at that exact moment haunted me for years. I was eight years old at a Little League Baseball game. There were rows of fields at that Rec Center, and you could see them all from the playground. I was playing with my little sister on the swing set, when I heard a yelp! I instantly recognized the screech as my mom, and turned to see what was going on. What I saw horrified me. My mom had been stung by a bee, and right in the middle of all the fields, she dropped her pants and went running. When my dad tried to console her, settle her down, and try to get her to put her pants back on, things got even worse. She fought him , slapped him ,and called him names that I had never heard before and hoped I would never hear again. What I felt was inexplicable. I was so embarrassed, I wanted to crawl into my skin and die. The kids and adults alike were all laughing, and it seemed like if eyes weren't on her, they were on me. They probably were not, but at the time you couldn't have convinced me of that. I was used to being embarrassed because of the way she acted but this took the cake. By 8 years old I was ashamed of who I was, embarrassed to be me. However, I never said a word. She was my mom after all, and I loved her, didn't I?

So whether it happened instantaneously, or snuck up on you over months or even years, it doesn't matter. What matters is that you are here now to try to learn how to cope, and ultimately, THRIVE. You are here to learn about what got you feeling the way you do, and how you can emerge stronger, more confident and well adjusted. Admitting that alcohol has taken over your life is a scary time and I am here to tell you that you are not alone. Right now, it is estimated that there are over 18 million children of alcoholics in the United States. That is 18 million children that are feeling, seeing and experiencing situations similar to yours. With the lock downs of the 2020 Covid pandemic, that number has been increasing steadily, and more children than ever are in need of help. The good news is that there is more help than ever out there, you just have to know where to look. I am here to help you find those resources, and get you to the support you need through this frightening and uncertain time.

AL-ANON OR ALATEEN

Now that you have accepted the fact that you need help in dealing with your situation, where should you go? While there are many support groups out there, my personal experience has been with Al-anon groups. As a teen, the group is called Alateen. Both work around the 12 Step program that was adopted by Alcoholics Anonymous back in 1935. They are spiritual programs focused on finding a higher purpose or power in order to recover from the effects someone's drinking has had on our lives. While it is based on the concepts of Alcoholics Anonymous, it differs in that it focuses on the people that are affected by the alcoholic and not the alcoholic him/herself. It focuses on working on you, as a person and not becoming completely consumed with the alcoholic.

It is NOT, unfortunately, going to give you a blue print or plan to get your alcoholic to stop drinking. I urge you not to let this discourage you, and I beg of you to look at this with an open mind. I attended an Alateen meeting at 13, and left angry and more confused than ever. I wanted to go in there and have them tell me in no uncertain terms, just what I had to do to keep my parents from drinking. I wanted the 12 steps to be steps such as....

1. Dump their liquor when they are not looking
2. Love them more so that they don't have to drink
3. Let them see that they love you more than they love alcohol so they don't want to drink, etc, etc, etc.

Those words never came. And I was mad. I was mad as hell. It wasn't until 20 years later, that I realized that my life was in shambles, and all the dysfunction of my childhood was here to stay unless I did something about it. That is when I attended an Al-anon meeting. (I was too old to go to Alateen at this point.) This time I did it with open ears and open eyes. I was willing to do just about anything to find just a moment of serenity, and progress towards a more "normal" life.

Meetings used to be in person only, now that is not the case. You can go to the app, **Al-Anon Family Groups**. There you will see a schedule of On-line meetings that you can attend any time. You can also find out where there are meetings in your area to attend in person by going to www.al-anon.org Some days I attend one, some days, if I am feeling a little sad, lonely or confused, I may attend as many as two or three. The choice is yours. However, I do suggest that you try at least six meetings before deciding. That seems to be the magic number, which turns skeptical bystanders into beginning believers.

Alateen has many quotes, slogans and phrases that I absolutely love. Among some of my favorites are:

"Let Go and Let God"

"One Day at a Time"

"Live and Let Live"

"Just for Today"

"Progress, Not Perfection"

"Let It Begin With Me"

"Easy Does It"

The one I like the best, and which you can apply to anything in this book is "Take what you love and leave the rest."

ABUSE

Abuse in any form to any human or animal in unacceptable. Yet it happens every day to millions of children around the world. So much of this abuse is because of addiction, the majority of it coming from alcoholism. For the purpose of giving you a general overview of abuse, we are going to discuss the four main types of abuse, specifically child abuse. If you are a victim of any types of this abuse, it is super important that you do something to help yourself TODAY! If it is not you, but someone that you know, it is also super important that you do something. If you are an educator, or work with children in any capacity, it is your responsibility and obligation to say something to someone. No form of abuse is to be tolerated, and should always be reported to the proper authorities. Fear of retaliation from the abuser often causes children to not speak up about their own abuse, so it is all of our jobs to keep a keen eye out, and to not accept any abuse as acceptable.

The Federal Child Abuse Prevention and Treatment Act (CAPTA) defines child abuse and neglect as, "any recent act or failure to act on the part of a parent or caretaker, which results in death, serious physical or emotional harm, sexual abuse or exploitation."[ii] This definition encompasses four basic types of abuse. They are physical abuse, psychological abuse, sexual abuse and neglect.

Physical abuse is often the one that alerts teachers and friends to the situation. Children come in with bumps, bruises, broken ribs, black eyes, and even more serious injuries. An alcoholic will often claim that they were just disciplining the child, or denying that the event happened at all. Discipline often crosses the line into abuse, especially when drinking escalates, tempers flare, and drunken blackouts become the norm. There are also less obvious forms of abuse that the alcoholic uses thinking that they will not be found out. My mother used to brush my long hair (Which was down to my butt) with a very stiff brush. She would brush so hard it would leave large lumps on my head that hurt so badly to the touch. They were all over my head. When I tried to call her out on it she just laughed. "They will never say I did anything wrong. All I did was brush your nasty knotty hair. They will never try to say I hurt you." They did notice the bumps when I was in the second grade. They had a lice epidemic in the elementary school I attended, and checked everyone's head. Not only did I have lice, but I also had large welts all over my head. Social services was called, she explained it away, the beatings were worse when they left, and I never mentioned it again. So not ALL forms of physical abuse are noticeable to the naked eye.

Sexual abuse is next. Unfortunately, stats say that one in four girls and one in six boys under the age of 18 will be sexually abused. And sadly, only 10 percent of these will be by strangers. That means that 90 percent of sexual abuse cases are from people that the child knows. Sexual abuse includes all form of sexual activity including, but not limited to incest, rape, fondling, touching, and sodomy. While it is not directly proven that children of alcoholics suffer more cases of sexual abuse, we do know two things. One is that excessive drinking causes a lack in judgement as well as heightened aggression in many people. This is turn could lend itself to there being more opportunities for the alcoholic to perform acts that they may normally not perform under more coherent conditions. The second thing we know is that victims of sexual abuse as children have a much higher risk of having addiction problems later in life. Either way we know that the long lasting effects of children that are sexually abused are severe.

The third form of child abuse is the least visible, but has some of the longest lasting long term effects. This is psychological abuse. Honestly, it even just sounds bad. Psychological or mental abuse. It is literally a parent or other adult using words and other non physical forms to diminish a child's self worth, self esteem, sense of identity. It becomes so bad in many cases that it negatively impacts the child's emotional development. This type of abuse is about control and power. They use words and actions that are very hurtful and damaging.

I remember the words that my mom used with me. I was fat, stupid, ugly, useless, unloved, not wanted, lazy, and puny. And that was just a normal Monday. At fifty three years old, when someone says something to me that makes me feel the way she made me feel, I literally feel like I am five years old again. I want to curl up in the corner with my teddy bear and cry. This type of abuse buries itself deep into your psyche and does damage that is hard to heal. Children begin to believe what is being said about them, often to the point that they don't even realize they are being abused. Because of this, they don't think to tell anyone or stick up for themselves.

The final type of abuse that we will talk about is another form of abuse that is often difficult to identify, mostly because there are not often physical signs. This is neglect. I will discuss neglect deeper later on in the book, but just want to touch on what it is, as one of the four types of abuse. Neglect is a type of abuse that is administered simply by a parent or caretaker not doing anything. They deny the child of basic needs. These needs may be physical needs, such as food, weather appropriate clothing or medical services. However, the neglect that really leaves a child suffering down the road is the emotional neglect. Caregivers deny children the basic psychological needs such as love, safety in their environment, and social interactions. This can have such a devastating effect on children, as severe neglect can actually change the way in which a child's brain develops, and affects their ability to process certain forms of information. Down the road this can lead to social,emotional, cognitive and behavioral disorders.

The good news is that there is hope for recovery from all forms of abuse and neglect. But again, and I know you are sick to death of hearing this... it will not be easy. Getting help early is the first step in the right direction, but there is a lot of work to do. To start with, the emotional effects of abuse and neglect need to be dealt with. The best tip I can give you right now to begin working on the new you is that you are going to have to be able to discredit the information you have been told and learn to love yourself.

I did a little exercise with a girl that came to me because her mom was violently emotionally abusive. She had such a low self esteem when she came to me, and I could see the pain in her face. The words that my mom had spoken to me had been spoken to her over and over and over again, for years. I had her do one little exercise which she said not only did she enjoy doing, but it made her feel a little better every day. It was nothing more than positive self affirmations....

When she heard "You are ugly" she said out loud "I am beautiful". When she heard "You are stupid" she yelled to herself "I am super smart." When she was told that her mom never wanted her to begin with, she responded "I am loved more than anyone in the world." She had to say it out loud and she had to do it EVERY time that a negative thought came to her, or someone said something to her that made her feel bad.

I ran into her a few months later, and the change was amazing. I asked how she was doing and she was gleaming. She talked about the exercise we had come up with together a few months back. She admitted that at first it felt wrong, and she did it quietly to herself. After a little while, she could say it out loud and not feel ashamed. After even a little more time, she began to have fun with it. She even learned to laugh at herself when she yelled out these positive affirmations wherever she was, no matter who was standing around. At about the two month mark, she said she didn't feel strange, embarrassed, or ashamed when she yelled out. By the time I talked to her six months later, she felt that she was actually the person she was yelling about.

While this was just a side note about a little experiment, it was not meant to derail from the subject of abuse. I just wanted to show you that while abuse is horrible and traumatic, and NEVER acceptable, it is something that you can survive. It can be damaging and hurtful and devastating in so many different ways. But it is the kind of damage that can be undone. You just have to make the choice that you want to start. You are in the right place to begin looking for answers, and you have an army of support that we can get you to! Remember, it is NEVER too early to start loving you!

BABYSTEPS

Okay. Now you've accepted that you need help and you've got a couple resources under your belt to start the healing process. I caution you to slow down. Getting to this point did not happen overnight. It may have taken days, weeks, months, or even years. For some, it has happened over their entire lives. This is not the section that talks about how in one minute you can make your life more enjoyable, safe, happy and calm. You just started this journey to happiness. It is going to take awhile to get there. We call them baby steps. Al-anon has a slogan that you will hear repeated several times. "ONE DAY AT A TIME". Right now you may be in the "One Hour At A Time" stage. That is ok. You have to learn to walk before you run, or in this case, deal before you heal. Knowing you are in a situation that can be helped is incredibly empowering, but you must not get ahead of yourself. Being that it possibly took years to get to the point that you are at, you must understand that it will take a lifetime of work to work the process. However, the good news is, it CAN be done, and every small step in the right direction is that much closer to the serenity you deserve.

So exactly where do you start? I encourage you to join some type of support group, scan the internet, gather as much information as you can, and then sit back and get ready for the healing journey of a lifetime. I host a Facebook page called Children of Alcoholics Thriving NOW! Every day there will be new tips, quotes and words of encouragement to read. It is also a place where you can voice your opinion, share stories, ask questions, and look for answers. The small group inside that page is private, and only myself and other children of alcoholics are allowed in there. Just like Alateen, you know that your information is safe and your anonymity will be protected. Just as in Alateen, what goes on in that group stays in that group. Being in a group of people that all understand what you are going through can be very comforting. There is no judgement, no condemnation, no ridicule. Just a bunch of teens inspiring each other through their own personal stories and victories, no matter how small.

Reading and writing are also great ways to start your journey. Journaling is a great form of self expression and also a great form of self discovery. When you write for even a ten or fifteen minute period, it gets you thinking about things sometimes in a way you never thought of them before. It gives you a chance to reflect in silence, and contemplate the past, present and future. You are invited to download a free printable Journal to accompany this book at www.tammyvincent.com It guides you through
52 writing prompts following the chapters in this book that will help you explore your feelings, and discover what questions you still have about what is going on in your life.

Jane couldn't help but feel that things were hopeless in the beginning. She said that she spent every moment thinking about how she could just make the situation better. She also said that it wasn't until she started going to AL-Anon, and really used the tools that they gave her, to really have a clear understanding about what she was facing, and how she could come out happy at the end of it. And she admitted that she knew it was going to take time, time, and more time.

BLACKOUTS

Me: "Mommy... why did you tell me that you hated me and that you wish I was never born?"

Alcoholic: "I never said such a thing. Why would I say that? I love you so much my little angel."

Me: "Oh, ok. I'm sorry."

I remembered those words spoken to me over and over again, it seemed like every day. Of course it was only when my mom was really drunk. When I asked my dad about it, he just said that she was drinking and didn't mean it. I remember thinking that I drank all the time, and it never made me hate anybody in my family. Of course that was the pure, innocent 6 year old thinking and understanding. "Drinking" in our household had become a bad word. One that we tried not to mention, because in my eyes, it made bad things happen and got me in trouble. I was often slapped, kicked and in other ways punished for things that I didn't even know I did. However, it still made me mad and confused. I was left wondering two things on those nights...1. Why does she hate me? And 2. Why does she lie and say she never said that? I didn't have a lot of guidance from either mom or dad in my very young years, but I did know that lying was bad, and we weren't allowed to do it.

And she must have been lying, I convinced myself, because there's no way she didn't remember saying those horrible things to me over and over.

It wasn't until much later on that I understood what a black out was. Has your alcoholic ever said or done something horrible when they were drinking and then deny it in the morning? Did it leave you confused and sad, and even a little scared? Most likely it left you feeling angry because you want them to admit what they said or did, and yet they stand there and lie to your face when confronted. Unfortunately, and fortunately, they may be telling the truth. They actually may not remember it at all. It is called an alcoholic blackout.

So, what exactly happens during an alcoholic blackout? There is a section in your brain called the hippocampus. It is where long term and short term memories are stored. During an alcoholic blackout, the hippocampus loses its "connection" and fails to move events from the short term to the long term memory. The long term memory is where we retrieve events, relive them and "remember" them. So, really, even though it seems almost impossible, during a blackout, these memories are not even being formed. [iii]

You're probably wondering exactly how much alcohol you have to drink to experience an alcoholic blackout. While it depends on the individual, alcoholic blackouts typically occur when a persons' Blood Alcohol Content reaches somewhere around .22, The legal limit for driving in most states is .08 , so a .22 is almost three times the legal limit. In short, the answer is quite a bit of alcohol.

There are basically two types of blackouts your alcoholic may experience. A complete alcoholic blackout occurs when they do not remember anything and even prompting or therapy can not bring those memories out. Literally, those events were never stored as memories. Then there is a fragmented blackout, where partial events and "bits and pieces" will be remembered. This is the most common type of blackout. It not only scares and confuses you as the recipient and witness of the events, but also does the same to the alcoholic. They wake up scared, confused and often ashamed at what they may have said or done. You will see later in the book why it seems as though I am being sympathetic to the alcoholic and his or her actions, but for right now, let's focus on what you should do about these events.

Dealing with these blackouts can be extremely scary. You may feel hurt and unloved when your alcoholic says or does things during a blackout. Should you confront them? That depends on the situation. Letting them know that what they said or did made you feel bad is not horrible, but remember that they may not remember doing it, and you could be met with a defensive and shameful attitude. Sometimes waiting a little bit may be the best bet, or just chalking it up to the fact that discussing it with them may be falling on deaf ears. Maybe at this point it is better to talk to someone in your support group that understands, and can give you the support you need in this uncertain time.

CAUSE, CURE AND CONTROL

(The 3 C's)

AA speaks often about the 3 C's of alcoholism and addiction. The 3 c's are Cause, Cure, Control. Accepting the 3 C's, and REALLY accepting them are crucial points in starting your healing.

"If you weren't such a pain, I wouldn't have to drink." "Living with you and your sister and brother makes me drink". "If I just had a better life I wouldn't want to drink".

Sound familiar? Ignore it, and ignore it, and ignore it. That is nonsense. While they don't really know what does cause alcohollism, they do know that one particular person or circumstance can in no way cause it, either. The guilt you are probably feeling after hearing those words is unnecessary and needs to be squashed. While there may be things in your life that you have a right to feel guilty about, causing your alcoholics disease is not one of them. I beg of you to release this belief and you will feel just a tiny bit of stress lifted from your shoulders. You are still a child, and do not deserve to carry the burden of causing a disease you have no control over.

So now that you know you didn't cause it, the next question must be "Can I cure it?" Unfortunately, you can not. There is no complete cure for alcoholism. Once you are an alcoholic, you will always be an alcoholic. Of course, an alcoholic can stop the active phase of alcoholism by remaining dry, but the disease still exists. Many alcoholics remain in recovery for decades, and may never drink again, but the disease still remains. It is during this time that the alcoholic will find better ways to deal with situations, past traumas, and life in general. Sadly, however, if you are looking for an easy way to cure this disease, as you can with other diseases, there is no real answer.

The final "C" word is control. Oh, boy, is that one I wish that I had a better grasp on. I wanted to control everything. My happiness, my siblings happiness, my parents' drinking. I learned quickly that I could not control one bit of an alcoholics' drinking and choices, no matter how hard I tried. I sure was going to try though. I spent the better part of my teen years trying to control every aspect of everything in our household. Looking back, I gave up what little freedom and happiness I did have as a child, spending that time trying desperately to control everything around me. I urge you to quickly grasp the concept that an alcoholics' recovery is not your problem and you can't control it. The only one who has control over their addiction is the alcoholic; and until they admit that they have a problem and want to get help, there is nothing that you can do.

Have you caught yourself pouring liquor down the drain, begging them to stop, or trying to be the absolute best person you can be so that they will not have a reason to drink? None of this will work. The only thing that will work for an alcoholic to stop drinking is for them to want them to stop. Because of that, it is vitally important that you focus on the things that you can control.

My favorite prayer, and one you will encounter many times in your journey to a happier, healthier you, is the serenity prayer.

"God grant me the serenity to accept the things I can not change, the courage to change the things I can. and the wisdom to know the difference"

So what can you control? While you may be stumped right now to think of anything, that is normal. Be creative. Think of ways to nurture you! You can control the activities that you join. You can control the amount of time you stay at home in that toxic environment. You can control being the best person you can be. You can control how you react to certain situations. You can control the people that you associate with. You can control your emotions. You can control your life outside of the home. The list literally goes on and on. Seek out support, I beg of you. If you don't want to go to an Alateen meeting, join a support group. Whatever you do, know that controlling the things in your life that you can is a key element in reaching that serenity and peace in your life that you so deserve.

To sum up the 3 C's... You did not cause your alcoholics' drinking, you can not cure their disease, and you can not control it. You must learn to adapt and cope and control the things that you can. It is a horrible disease, which affects everyone involved, and the more you do to control the things you can, the happier you will be in the long run.

DISEASE

In the last section, you heard it mentioned several times the word disease. Alcoholism is without a doubt, a disease. It was classified as a disease in 1956, by the American Medical Association. They made this determination based on the fact that excessive alcohol use affects both the structure and function of the brain. Unfortunately, it is a very difficult disease to understand. There are several names for alcoholism, and for the purpose of stories and examples, we will use the terms interchangeably. Alcoholism, alcohol use disorder, alcohol abuse, and just plain "Having a drinking problem" are a few of the terms that are used. Basically it means the same thing… The person has established a pattern of alcohol use and misuse to the point that there are now problems and negative consequences in the persons' life. These problems can include health, mental issues, financial, family problems and legal troubles just to name a few. Which one of these, if any, has your alcoholic had to face? The fact that you are here reading today means that for sure we can conclude that at the very least , the family dynamic is being affected. Am I right?

Does knowing that your parent has a disease make it any better for you? It didn't for me. While I tried to wrap my head around the fact that it was a disease, and they could not help it, I didn't feel any better,. It literally took me until my mid thirties, and many years in Al-Anon meetings before I was able to understand that my parents couldn't help themselves any more than they could help from having cancer or some other debilitating disease. Would you be mad at your alcoholic if they came home and said that they had cancer? Absolutely not! You would find every way in the world to try to help them and make their lives easier and more comfortable. Alcoholism is no different. This was the hardest thing for me to understand. My thinking was always that alcoholics had a choice. They chose to drink and they chose to hurt me and they chose to continue to do the one thing that they know did the most significant and devastating damage to me, our home and everyone around us. That is what I thought for over 30 years. I was wrong... Dead wrong. An alcoholic has no more control over their drinking than a diabetic has over the fact that they don't produce insulin. While they can get help for their alcoholism, getting angry at them for this disease is not going to help. In the long run, it will only make you, and them, feel worse.

Again, you are probably asking if this is supposed to make you feel better? It does not feel any better I am certain. This is why we are here together. To understand the disease of alcoholism and find ways to cope with the disease, and its horrific effects. You may want to yell and scream, and that's ok. My goal for you and anybody else reading this is that we work together to discover ways to deal with this disease; most importantly focusing on you as an individual, not the alcoholic. I am not asking you to forgive them immediately, or pretend that the things that happened to you, and continue to happen to you don't exist. I only want to educate you, as much as possible, so that yo can have the necessary tools to deal with what life will continue to throw at you.

Understanding that alcoholism is a disease, and not a character flaw of your parent is a very big step towardsstarting to heal. Understandably, it is a very difficult step. I mentioned that it took me over 30 years to fully believe in my heart that it was a disease that they couldn't beat, but once Idid I looked at my entire life very differently. I knew that while I could not do anything about my alcoholics drinking,I understood that I needed to help myself.

DETACHMENT

When you hear the word detachment, what do you think? Does the vision of running away come into your mind? Or refusing to talk to your alcoholic when they've been drinking, and then punishing them for days with the silent treatment? Does the thought of never having to speak to them again appeal to you? Seems fair to me, right? After all, their use of alcohol, and the results of their drinking has made you endure verbal, physical, and unfortunately sometimes even sexual abuse that was all caused from their drinking.

It only seems natural that the form of detachment that would be best for everyone would be total and complete detachment from the "Problem person" in general. Unfortunately, not only is that a drastic and sometimes unrealistic scenario to play out, but it doesn't help anyone. When we speak of detachment based on most 12 step programs, the term detachment has been changed to "detachment with love".

What exactly does detachment with love mean? According to Hazelden Betty Ford Foundation, detachment with love means caring enough about others to allow them to learn from their mistakes. It means stepping away so that you are not completely engrossed in their lives and their problems. It means walking away sometimes so that you can focus on your own life, instead of a disease that you have absolutely no control over. When you stay and try to control things, , which doesn't work anyway, you remain stressed and anxious. You live a life constantly in the middle of chaos, uncertainty and violence, When you learn to detach with love, two things happen. First, you get a chance to care for yourself. The time spent away from the house enables you to make friends, form connections with others outside of your chaotic household, and hopefully get to see a sense of normalcy that you are probably yearning to experience. At the same time, it allows your alcoholic the opportunity to discover life without someone jumping to the rescue all the time. It allows them the experience of having to deal with the consequences of their actions without assistance. While this may seem cruel and heartless, it is actually quite the opposite. What is the end goal to you? To have your alcoholic stop drinking? If so, the one and only way that this is going to happen is for them to want to stop drinking. And no matter how vicious and unloving it seems to watch a loved one get themselves into trouble, this is often what they need. Having to deal with the consequences of their action at some point may just be the straw that broke the camels back, so to speak. In order to want to go up, you sometimes have to hit rock bottom first. Detaching with love is a way to inadvertently, or "accidentally" cause that.

ENABLING

Do any of the following statements hit a nerve, or sound way too familiar to you?

- ➤ You make excuses for your parent when they act or behave irresponsibly
- ➤ You call in sick to work for them when they are too hungover to get up
- ➤ You help your parent get hold of alcohol when they are out, even if it means taking them to the store yourself
- ➤ You ignore or tolerate problematic behavior
- ➤ You interfere so that your alcoholic parent doesn't have to suffer the consequences of their actions
- ➤ You sacrifice your own needs for the needs of everyone else, including your alcoholic parent
- ➤ You take on more than your fair share of responsibilities around the house, or …
- ➤ You simply do NOTHING AT ALL, like the problem doesn't exist.

The list, I'm sure, goes on and on. Now, take a deep breath and think about all the things you just read. Maybe even try to think of other ways that you enable your alcoholic parent on a daily basis.

Did you add to the list? Most students that I talk to in your situation can think of dozens of specific examples of how they enabled their alcoholic parent, almost always meaning to do the right thing. When you really think about it though, do you feel that this is this is helping or hurting the situation in the long run? I'm sure it did not start in a malicious way. You thought that you were helping, or keeping them out of trouble. You were doing it to be kind, keeping the peace and not making waves. It makes total sense to act that way for the ones we love. We do not want to see them suffer, be hurt, or get in trouble. So we jump in and do what we think is best at that time, in that situation. We try to provide support, help, compassion and answers for the people we love, especially when they are feeling down. However, enabling is only keeping them down in the long run.

The long term effects of enabling are crippling for the alcoholic. What is it that you want more than anything in your life? You want your parent to stop drinking and continue to stay sober, right? As we mentioned earlier, there is only one thing that is going to make the alcoholic quit drinking, and that is for them to WANT to quit! And when you make it easy for them to act the way they do with absolutely no consequences for their actions, why would they want to do anything different?

Jamie remembers constantly calling her moms boss and explaining that she didn't feel well and couldn't come in to work. It was ironically always the day after Jamie had spent the night holding back her mother's hair while she vomited up all the contents of her stomach, and just hours after she had tucked her in to bed, shoes and all.

"It wasn't until I set some boundaries and refused to call her boss, that things took a turn for the better.

Mom almost lost her job after I refused to do her dirty work. While we thought it was the end of the world, and we didn't know what to expect, it all turned out alright. Her boss helped get her into a rehab facility and she is now twelve years sober. Had I continued to enable her, I really believe she would still be drinking today."

As with most of the topics in this book, the topic of enabling could be its own book. However, for the sake of simplicity, and just to give you an introduction, what is important for you, as the child of an alcoholic to know, is that until you let your alcoholic be forced to take care of themselves, things will never get better. Right now, during this time, the person that you should be most worried about taking care of is yourself! Just a reminder you are #1!

EMPATHY

Empathy: "The capacity to understand or feel what another person is experiencing from their frame of reference", or simply put "To be able to put yourself in someone else's shoes"

This is one of the toughest sections of the book for me to write. One, because it was the toughest part of my journey to understand. Two, I can not even fathom trying to have really understood it as a child. When I was deep in the throes of hurt, pain, abuse, despair and anguish, if someone had told me that the best thing for my alcoholic parent was for me to be empathetic to their situation, I would have wanted to spit on them. That is how angry I was. The thought of someone telling me to reach deep within my soul and "Put myself in their shoes, and try to understand what they are going through" still honestly, gives me a sick feeling in my stomach. Especially when I think back to so many frightening times I had as a child. Understanding how a mother who was supposed to love their children could be so cruel just made no sense to me.

I was 13 years old when someone said that it was beneficial for the children of alcoholics to be empathetic to the parents situation. (Ironically that was told to me at that fateful Alateen meeting that ran me off for over two decades.) It was explained to me that while the natural tendency for people is to judge and condemn, an alcoholic feels shame without anyone pointing it out to them. What they really need is someone on their side who is willing to sit beside them and feel the pain with them. Of course it is impossible for someone who has never been in the grips of addiction to completely feel what it feels like, but making the alcoholic feel that you understand what they're going through is huge.

I also want to clarify the difference between sympathy and empathy. Sympathy is the pity or sorrow you feel for someone's misfortune or bad circumstance. This differs from empathy in that when you have empathy, you actually get in someone else's head and feel the emotions they are feeling. It does not help to just feel sorry, but to actually make them believe you care.

Now that you understand what empathy is, do you think its possible to feel empathy toward your alcoholic parent? Next to an impossible task, I'm sure you are thinking. I remember the day I tried to be empathetic to my mom (who passed away when I was 18). I pictured the first event that came to mind, and tried,

unsuccessfully to put myself in her shoes.....

"Hit her! Hit her! For God sakes, hit her!" It was me screaming at my dad. It was 3 in the morning and my parents were fighting as they always did. Mom called my brother and me down to "witness the beating".

"See what your father does to me when you guys are sleeping? He hits me. Over and over, he hits me." And then she did the unimaginable. She turned and without warning dug her lit cigarette into his arm, holding it tight so that the lit butt did maximum damage. I could smell the hair burn on his arm, and see the hole in his arm that the cigarette had caused. And he didn't even flinch. He never batted an eye.

"Linda, I will not give you the satisfaction. Go back to bed, kids." The shock, horror and humiliation on my father's face was almost more than I could handle. I wanted him to hit her so badly. I wanted to hit her. I wanted somebody to stop the insanity. But everyone just stood there in shock, afraid to move. Afraid that the first person to move would take the brunt of the situation.

Many years later, I finally understood what she was doing that night. It was the mid 70's, and my parents were getting ready to go through a nasty divorce. There would be a custody battle for sure, and my mom was trying to get my dad to hit her in front of us. She thought that would be the only way to show that she was the better parent, and gain custody. It was manipulative, and horrific, and just another example of how messed up the alcohol had made her. In her mind, she was doing whatever she had to do to make sure that she did not lose her family, the one and only thing that she thought she had left. Now I understood. But did I understand when I was a child? Absolutely not. If you are having trouble with this, that is completely normal. It is not expected that this is going to be an easy task.

Feeling empathy towards a person that is hurting you so badly is never an easy task. It will take a lot of work, and a lot of support. I encourage you to try. My mother died before I could spend even one moment having empathy for her, and that makes me truly sad. Trying to have empathy is yet another step toward not only a more peaceful and cooperative relationship with your parent, but also your own recovery and serenity. There are a few suggestions I can make that may help you practice this art, and I encourage you to practice them on a daily basis.

1. Focus on your similarities with someone, not their differences. This tends to keep you from being judgmental, since judging them would be judging yourself

2. Immerse yourself into someone else's life when you observe their behavior. Try to really imagine what it feels like to be in their shoes. Use all of your senses and imagine you are there. Smell what they smell, feel what it feels like. Hear from a different set of ears. Visualization is a very powerful tool

3. Don't just listen, share as well. Listening to someone is super important, but sometimes opening up about your own life, and sharing your own thoughts with someone will help you build an empathetic and trusting relationship

4. Ask questions. Even though you may think that you know someone and what they're feeling, digging in and asking questions not only shows you care, but gives you more information than you had before. You may think that you know what they're thinking, but you probably don't

5. Watch movies and read fiction and practice putting yourself in people's shoes. It is not a skill learned immediately, and the more you practice, the better you will be at it.

6. DO NOT JUDGE. Talk and listen to both verbal and nonverbal cues, and do so without judgement. Being empathetic on a regular basis will make you a much happier and less judgmental person in the long run.

Great Quotes on Empathy

"Learning to stand in somebody else's shoes, to see through their eyes, that's how peace begins. And it's up to you to make that happen. Empathy is a quality of character that can change the world." – Barack Obama

"Leadership is about empathy. It is about having the ability to relate to and connect with people for the purpose of inspiring and empowering their lives." – Oprah Winfrey

"Could a greater miracle take place than for us to look through each other's eyes for an instant?" – Henry David Thoreau

"Empathy is about finding echoes of another person in yourself." – Mohsin Hamid

"There is a nobility in compassion, a beauty in empathy a grace in forgiveness." – John Connolly

FAMILY

When we say that alcoholism is a family disease, we truly mean it. When there is an alcoholic in the family, whether it be one, two, or all of them, every single person is affected. Does it affect everyone the same? Absolutely not. Every single person is affected differently. It may depend on how the alcoholic treats you. It may depend on how you react to the alcoholism. It may depend on your age, your gender, or your position in the family. There's so many different variables that affect how we react to our circumstances. The only thing we know for absolutely sure is that NO ONE escapes being affected in some one. NO ONE! I, myself, had a younger sister and an older brother. I was in the middle. Not the baby, not the oldest. The way that the three of us reacted and acted was 100 % different. Our perceptions of what was happening and what we had to do to survive were totally different. And now, thinking back about it, the one thing that we all had in common in how we reacted is that we didn't talk about it. I remember reacting to the individual events, but never once do I remember having a private conversation with either my brother or my sister as to what was happening. We didn't even have the knowledge, or strength or whatever we needed to even talk amongst ourselves about the horror that was right there in our home. We took the expression, "Don't talk, don't tell, don't feel" to the fullest extent, even with the ones we probably could have counted on the most for support and understanding. It's definitely one of the points that hit the hardest with me when I finally starting opening up and talking about what happened in our home. My advice to you is that if you do have siblings, please talk to them, if you have any kind of relationship at all.

So, back to the topic at hand... The family disease. While we now understand that this disease affects everybody in different ways, it is important to understand the different roles that children growing up with this type of dysfunction will most likely adapt. They have many similar descriptions and names, but at the end of the day, there are five basic roles.

Do any of these sound familiar to you? Do you fall into one of these types of children more than another? Knowing which role you play in the family may help you in the long run so that you can learn different skills, thought patterns and ways to incorporate healthy behaviors into the family dynamics. Remember, in many ways you become the addict that you live with. Remember, too, that the person that you have developed into is in no way right or wrong. It is 100% exactly what can and should be expected to happen after what you have been through, and are continuing to go through now. Besides the addict themselves, here are the five basic family roles.

1. The enabler, or caretaker... This person steps in and takes care of the alcoholic, often minimizing or fixing the problem. They make excuses for the alcoholic, and often clean up messes for them. While the idea probably started just trying to reduce the anxiety and stress in the situation, the opposite happens. By failing to let the

41

alcoholic suffer the consequences of his/her actions, they are often led deeper and deeper into the destructive and self-sabotaging life.

2. The Scapegoat… This is the person that generally takes the blame for what happens in the family. They are often the middle child. Sadly, they feel that they are deserving of taking that blame, and often take it so that the alcoholic and other family members do not have to suffer those feelings of blame. Unfortunately, this is way too much for a child to endure and they usually end up so angry that they "lose their shit". They are often in enough trouble to take some of the negative attention off of the alcoholic. With this pent up anger, the scapegoat often lashes out by either getting in trouble with the law, picking the wrong friends, or acting out sexually, with little regard for themselves.

3. The Hero, Perfectionist, or Overachiever…. This person generally does everything in their power to make the family look good, and "Normal". They think that the appearance of a perfect world will keep people in the dark. They are often the oldest children. They adapt to the stress of the family by becoming super competent in everything that they do. Because they feel that they are the leaders of the family, and responsible for everyone's happiness, they are often under an extreme amount of pressure, and turn to alcohol and drugs to calm the anxiety.

4. The Mascot…. This is the child that uses humor to diffuse situations. They believe that being funny, or joking around will calm the tension that normally exists in the house. They are often the youngest child, and realize at a very early age that laughing and joking lightens the mood

42

of the house. They typically are the center of attention, taking

the focus off of the alcoholic and can usually be seen laughing, joking, being silly, and especially making jokes about themselves. While it seems cute and funny at the time, these children are usually very confused, sad, lonely and very insecure. While they appear to be good at diverting the glum mood of the house, they rarely allow themselves to honestly feel their emotions until much later.

5. The lost child... This is the child that just simply seems to disappear. They don't do anything wrong, so there is no attention on them. They are often the youngest of the siblings. They cope with stressful situations by withdra-wing into themselves and detaching themselves from a group. They often engage in single person activities, with little interaction with other family members. Because of this, they have trouble forming any lasting relationships, and have a hard time communicating.

As I mentioned, none of these roles are bad. They JUST ARE. Taking a good look at where you fit into your family dynamics can be a start to becoming more well adjusted, healthier and happier. The internet offers way more information on each family role and even different ways of learning to cope. Research and knowledge of your individual situation are going to be key to your recovery. I encourage daily reading. I also encourage you to ask questions when you can, to whomever you feel that you can trust enough to talk to. Right now it is probably not your alcoholic, or even the non-drinking parent. Alateen, NACOA, your church, counselors, teachers and other family members are great resources. I can't encourage you enough to do whatever is in your power to start acquiring the tools that are available to you.

GRATITUDE

Gratitude is defined as a **conscious**, positive emotion that one can express when feeling thankful for something, whether that thing is tangible, or intangible. It seems like such a simple concept. To feel thankful, to be thankful, to appreciate what you have. Unfortunately, if you are reading this book, you may be going through days and weeks and even years where you just don't have a feeling of gratitude on your heart. How can you be grateful when your mother has taken away your food for the day? How can you be grateful when your father has locked you in your room for days? How can you be grateful when every time you turn around all you experience is loneliness, sadness and loss? While it may be hard to imagine, I am here to tell you that without a doubt, finding a feeling of gratitude may be the best home therapy you could give yourself.

The feeling of gratitude has so many different benefits. In general, it is associated with an overall general feeling of happiness. When practiced (yes, I said practiced) on a regular basis, gratitude has been known to have several positive effects. Here are just a few:

1. It makes us happier
2. It reduced stress

3. It helps us sleep better
4. It improves our friendships
5. It improves our physical health
6. It helps us be more resilient
7. It helps us be more kind
8. It helps improve self esteem
9. It improves relationships
10. It improves our mental strength

There are just a few of the benefits I have found, and the easiest ones to understand. Sounds great, right? But what if right now, as you sit here, you feel that you have too much to worry about and so little to be thankful for? That is where the practice comes in. I told you in the beginning that it was going to require some work on your end. I was not kidding.

If you noticed in the definition of gratitude it was said that it was a "Conscious, positive emotion." The key word here is "conscious". That means that it does not always come naturally. It has to be thought about and purposefully worked into your daily routine. However, I can tell you that as soon as I started practicing gratitude, my whole outlook on life got a little better. I started appreciating the things that I had, and stopped fretting about the things that had gone wrong. It was also very humbling to me, as my problems didn't seem nearly as big when I was thankful for the little things I had.

So exactly how do you practice gratitude? It's not like you just wake up one day and decide you are going to be thankful for everything in your life. It takes practice and discipline. I started doing this about five years ago, after I had come back from a conference. I was determined to do everything that they showed me, and I committed that day. Here are some of the tricks that I used to help myself become more grateful, and ultimately, happier.

Steps to Practicing Gratitude:

1. Wake up in the morning and immediately say thank you for what you have. If nothing else, I wake up and say "Thank you God for giving me another day", or "Thank you for a restful nights sleep". Then as I go through my morning routine, I literally say "Thank you God" for at least a dozen things. Not slipping in the shower, not running out of toothpaste, having toilet paper when I needed it... Well, you get the idea. It doesn't matter how big or small things are, just that you are grateful for them.

2. Take a walk outside and just enjoy the outdoors. Appreciate the small things and be grateful they are there. A butterfly, a puppy in the backyard, even a brand new bud on a bush that just came back to life after a long winter.

3. Tell someone you care about that you are thankful for them in your life. It may be a best friend, relative, or sibling. Watch the look on their face when you say it. Sometimes you are not the only one with sadness in your heart and a kind word can go a long way.

4. Meditate. Meditating, or just being still and taking the time to breathe is known to lower heartrate, reduce stress, and provoke a sense of positivity.

5. Minimize the negative thoughts. This is the one that was hard for me, but one that made the most difference when I embraced it. People now tell me I'm the most positive

person they know. That positivity is contagious. Watch how you start to attract positive people. So many examples come to mind when I'm driving. If someone cuts me off in traffic I am thankful that they didn't hit me, as well as being thankful they will get to work or wherever they are in such a hurry to get to, on time. If someone sits too long at a light when it turns green I am thankful that I got to rest for just another moment. My husband goes absolutely nuts in the car, complaining about everything and everyone. No wonder drives with him are so stressful. And, it's no wonder that we always get stuck in large lines and lots of traffic when he is driving…. "What you think about you bring about". Just saying.

6. Keep a gratitude journal. We will discuss later why journaling can be so powerful, but for now we will just discuss what keeping a gratitude journal does. When you put something in writing, it sinks into your head as the truth. If you reread your gratitude journal every day with ideas and things you are grateful for, you will reengage that positive mindset and reintroduce the feeling of gratitude every day.

7. Go through the motions of being grateful. To do this may mean thanking someone for something out loud, smiling to someone who is nearby, and even writing short notes to people that you are grateful. Again, even if you can't deliver this note for whatever reason, putting it down on paper makes it seem more real.

8. Use your senses… this one works especially well when you are having a tough time, and don't see anything obvious on the horizon to feel grateful for. Close your

eyes and go through each sense. Smell what you can smell. Is it the Downey fabric softener in the laundry room? Be grateful that you have clean clothes to wear. Hear the sounds around. SO you hear a bird? Be thankful that you are able to go outside whenever you want and just enjoy nature. Taste in your mind your favorite thing to eat and then treat yourself. Be thankful that you have the means to have that tasty treat, when others are not so lucky. Go through every sense until you are filled with small things to be grateful for. If any stick out profoundly, write them down in your gratitude journal, since next time these thoughts will be easier to manifest.

9. And last but not least, PRACTICE EVERY SINGLE OPPORTUNITY YOU CAN . I can not say this enough. It is a muscle memory and the more you put these strategies into practice the more it will be second nature. I promise you it will lead to a more positive and hopefully existence for you, improving relationships, self esteem, and overall happiness and joy.

Some of My Favorite Gratitude Quotes:

"When I pray, I always thank Mother Nature for all the beauty in the world. It's about having an attitude of gratitude" – Miranda Kerr

"I think gratitude is a big thing. It puts you in a place where you are humble" – Andra Day

"Living in a state of gratitude is the gateway to grace" – Arriana Huffington

"It is not joy that makes us grateful. It is gratitude that brings us joy" – David Steindl Rast

"Even in the chaos of life, moments of gratitude remind us to hold onto the good things" – Brit Morin

"The struggle ends when the gratitude begins" – Neale Donald Walsh

GOD

In this day and age, it is crazy that we are not supposed to mention God. It has almost, and it sickens me, become the "G" word. You can't bring it into schools, you have to be careful about who you offend, blah blah blah. When I began writing this book, I mentioned how much of my own recovery has been because of my relationship w i t h God. I talked passionately about how my bible studies and devotional books literally helped pull me out of a hell that I had been in for years. I was "Encouraged" not to talk about it. People told me just to mention and reiterate the fact that Al-anon refers to God as "The God of our understanding". Well, the GOD OF MY UNDERSTANDING, whose existence is non-negotiable in my heart and soul, will not be "Downplayed", as people suggested. What I will remind you is a quote from Al-anon, that says to "Take what you love and leave the rest".If you feel that you may be offended by my telling you about my personal journey with God, please skip to the next section of the book! I'll see you back in a few minutes.

For the people that do want to read on, I am glad you are here. Our God is a loving God, and definitely has our best interest at heart. However, there was a time it got so bad, I lost my faith. At the heart of my despair, I turned my back on God. I gave up on believing that He was on my side, or had a great plan for me. I was selfish and self centered and self absorbed, It was all about me, but honestly, at eight years old, who could blame me? All I could think at that time was "Why me? What did I do wrong? Why don't you love me? Why do you let her hit me? Why don't you save me? If you really were a loving God, you would make her stop!"

I was eight years old, hiding in the tiny little crawlspace between my brothers room and the attic. It was my safe place where I went when I really didn't want to be found. The area I lay in was about 18 inches high and I could barely breathe. It was uncomfortable, and dark, but not breathing was the goal. If I breathed, I might be heard, and ultimately found. This night was no different. She did hear me, she did find me, she did beat me. The second my dad walked out the door, she went looking. She needed to take out the anger on someone. The alcohol made her sooooo angry. In his mind, him leaving for a bit diffused the situation and returned the house to our "Normal"; kids in their rooms, Mom passed out on the couch. It wasn't until 36 years later that I finally admitted to my father what happened when he would sneak out of the house for some peace and quiet. I understood that he, too, deeply needed that quiet, so back then, I never said a word.

That particular night something in me snapped. I was so scared and angry and filled with hate. I could not understand how God could let this happen. How an eight year old could get beaten with a belt just for being. I gave up my God for almost two decades. I remained "Spiritual" in my own belief, but I didn't turn to my God for the help and understanding that I longed for. I thought I could do it all on my own. Wrong! I was dead wrong!

Now I look back and I see that God did have a plan for me. He did protect me. The proof is that I am still here. And now I'm here with a story. A story of survival, and resilience, and a love for God that is unstoppable. They always say that there is no testimony without a test. I have survived the test, and now with a refreshed and overdue love for Our Father, I have a testimony to share. It comes in the form of this book.

When things seem bleak and you are alone, confused or scared, read and reread these scriptures, and it will make you feel better. I am fifty three years old, and I still read them to this day.

Scripture that never fails me.....

"Don't fear because I am with you: don't be afraid for I am your God. I will strengthen thee; I will help thee; I will hold you with my righteous strong hand." Isaiah 41:10

"Be strong and courageous, Do not be afraid; Do not be discouraged, for the Lord your God will be with you wherever you go." Joshua 1:9

"Trust in the Lord with all your Heart, and lean not on your own understanding." Proverbs 2:5

"And we know that all things work together for good to them that love God, to them who are the called according to his purpose." Romans 8:28

"Casting all your anxieties on him, because he cares for you." Peter 5:7

"For I know the plans I have for you," declares the Lord. "Plans to prosper you and not harm you, plans to give you hope and a future." Jeremiah 29:11

"But the fruit of the Spirit is love, joy, peace, patience, kindness, goodness, faithfulness," Galatians 5:22

"I can do all things through Christ who strengthens me." Philippians 4:13

HIGHER POWER

Before we can begin this chapter, we first have to talk about the 12 steps of Al-anon and Alateen. While I mentioned back in section "A" that I highly recommend you attend these meetings and see what they are about, I never really gave you a real idea as to the beliefs that dictate their program. I must also share them with you so that you see how big the emphasis on spirituality is. I am going to simply list them, and then we will discuss the concept of a higher power.

Al-Anon and Alateen 12 Steps

Step 1: We admitted we were powerless over alcohol- that our lives had become unmanageable

Step 2: Came to believe that a Power greater than ourselves could restore us to sanity.

Step 3: Made a decision to turn our will and our lives over to the care of God as we understood him.

Step 4: Made a searching and fearless moral inventory of ourselves.

Step 5: Admitted to God, to ourselves and to another human being the exact nature of our wrongs.

Step 6: Were entirely ready to have God remove all these defects of character.

Step 7: Humbly asked Him to remove our shortcomings.

Step 8: Made a list of all persons we had harmed, and became willing to make amends to them all.

Step 9: Make direct amends to such people wherever possible , except when to do so would injure them or others.

Step 10: Continued to take personal inventory and when we were wrong promptly admitted it.

Step 11: Sought through prayer and meditation to improve our conscious contact with God as we understood Him, praying only for knowledge of His will for us and the power to carry that our.

Step 12: Having had a spiritual awakening as the result of these steps, we tried to carry this message to others, and to practice these principles in all our affairs. [iv]

Wow! That's a lot to throw at you like that. I get it. Does the thought of a 12 step program scare you in general? How many different emotions are going through your head right now??? While I really want to know, and dig in with you, it is not the time. Right now we are strictly dealing with the concept of a Higher Power. It does not have to be God, (although for me it is) My God is my higher power. Yours may be different. But whatever that higher power is, I urge you to figure it out. Take just a second and close your eyes and really think about who or what your higher power might be. Do you believe in God? If so, it's easy. God is your Higher Power. However, if you are unsure, or you don't believe in God, that's ok. Even Al- anon refers to God as "The God Of Your Understanding".

What makes you feel good? What do you look for when you are hurting, struggling, lost, confused and tormented? What do you think has a power that is greater than yours? Is it the Buddah, The Universe, The Sun, Mother Nature, Allah? What is something that is personal to you, and something that you know has a power higher than you? Picture that thing, and it is your Higher Power. Now isn't it great to have someone or something we can turn to in those times of need? Isn't it empowering to know that your Higher Power will take control of the things you have no control over.

Ok, so now we know that there is this Higher Power, and you're pretty sure you know what or who yours is. This Higher Power is omniscient (all knowing) Omnipresent (all present) and Omnipotent (all powerful) What exactly are the benefits of believing in such a thing?

Benefits of Believing In A Higher Power:

1. You understand and believe that you have, and never will, have any control over so many things in your life. You can now turn that control over to your HP
2. You are better able to cope when bad things happen
3. Since you know you are not in control of what's happening or going to happen, you tend to live more in the moment instead of fearing the future
4. You are set free of the daily worry of every tiny issue
5. Your spirituality is cultivated, and in the spiritual part of the mind is where healing begins
6. You suffer less anxiety
7. You live longer since stress and anxiety are known to shorten your lifespan

8. Ultimately, having a Higher Power gives you something for you to belong to. You are no longer alone. You just need to tap into what you think that your Higher Power wants you to do!

Practice these small tricks to connecting to your Higher Power:

1. Journal: I've mentioned the power of writing things down. When you write, take the time to reflect
2. Be open minded- Listen to what others have to say about different topics and then reflect, and make up your own decision about the situation
3. Pray: Just talk to your higher power. Form a relationship with that Higher Power, and engage with them. And to form a GREAT relationship with your Higher Power, do not just pray when things are bad. Pray and be thankful when things are good.
4. Serve others: When you put yourself out there and serve other people, you realize that the world is bigger than you and it humbles you and makes you realize your situation may not be as horrible as you think it is.
5. Enjoy nature... When you take the time to enjoy nature, you will be in awe of the beauty around you. Take a walk, nap by a pond or river. Enjoy the peace and quiet and just enjoy the HERE AND NOW!
6. Meditate: Preferably in nature. The two together are soooo powerful. Just a quiet moment alone with no cell phone, no video games, no noise helps you reflect and just listen to your heart. The things you need to hear will be revealed to you

Start today and just practice ways to connect with the spiritual you! It is a great place to be! Peace, serenity and zen all occur when you have a relationship with your Higher Power.

HOPE

When you hear the word "hope", what do you think? Do you feel doomed to a life where none of your hopes and dreams come true, or do you feel optimistic and hopeful about the future? I know how I felt at your age, and I can only imagine what is going through your head right now. Fortunately, there is a place for hope in your world, and you are becoming more equipped with tools to become once again hopeful.

Hope, by definition, is the desire and belief that there is something better in the future. The key words, of course, being desire and belief. That means you have to want to have a better future, and you have to believe that it is possible. That means, my friends, that we are going to have to buckle down and do some hard work. How you arrive at a mindset of hopefulness is going to be in part, a lot up to you. It will, however, determine a large part of your future happiness. Right now, while living in our own version of personal hell, having hope can seem unrealistic. Usually you are just trying to get through another day without pain, brutality, shame and suffering. But I can promise you, hope is on the horizon. Reading devotionals and a daily quote can give you a good dose of positivity. Reading books on hope can help. It is all about mindset and how you get there. Do you like to read?

Grab a devotional about Hope. Do you like to surf the internet? Join support groups that give you that daily dose of positivity. You can join us on Facebook at Children of Alcoholics Thriving Now, where teens and adults share stories. There will be daily positive quotes posted there. It is also a great place to vent your feelings, as members will more often than not respond with words of encouragement and hope. At the end of the day, your attitude can determine your success.

So what are some tricks to feel hopeful when living in a chaotic and uncertain world?

1. Consciously argue with yourself about what you are feeling hopeless about. Even talking it out loud sometimes makes it seem more doable for you. EX: I will never be able to have a normal life while mom is at home: Your response to yourself... Never is a long time. If I focus on me, and my own happiness, eventually I will be grown and happy and out of this house.

2. Visualize that good things are already happening. Sometimes it is enough to just visualize yourself in a better place, a better situation. The mind is a extremely powerful , and while visualizing isn't a cure all, it is certainly effective. Positive visualization will raise dopamine (the feel good hormone) levels instantly.

3. Express your feelings. When you release negative emotions, it can be healing. If you do not have a friend or family member that you feel comfortable sharing with, write them down in a journal. Once you write them down, picture them gone and try to replace them with something good that could happen in the future.

4. Practice gratitude. This is a recurring theme throughout this book, but one that is important. Very important. When you wake in the morning, thank your higher power for five things that you are grateful for. When you appreciate and are thankful for things in your life, it makes it seem more believable that there will be more circumstances in the future to be grateful for .

5. Set a small goal for something you want in the future. It doesn't have to be huge, just something you want to accomplish. Now brainstorm ways to reach that goal, and everything you need to do to get there. Push out any self-limiting thoughts as to why you can't and replace them with positive thoughts about why you of course, CAN!

While these suggestions may seem a bit cliché, they are worth a shot. Absolutely everything you do in a positive manner is ultimately leading you to a more happy, healthy, hopeful you.

Quotes for a More Hopeful You!

"All the great things are simple, and many can be expressed in a single word: Freedom, Justice, Honor, Duty, Mercy and Hope" – Winston Churchill

"The very least you can do in your life is figure out what you hope for. And the most you can do is live inside that hope. Not admire it from a distance, but live right in it, under its roof," – Barbara Kingsolver

"Hope can be a powerful force. Maybe there's no actual magic in it, but when you know what you hope for most and hold it like a light within you, you can make things happen, almost like magic." – Laini Taylor

"May the God of hope fill you with all joy and peace as you trust in him, so that you may overflow with hope by the power of the Holy Spriit." – Romans 15:13

"They say a person needs just three things to be truly happy in this world: someone to love, something to do, and something to hope for." – Tom Bodett

"Hope is important because it can make the present moment less difficult to bear. If we believe that tomorrow will be better, we can bear a hardship today." – Thich Nhat Hanh

"Learn from yesterday, Live for today, Hope for tomorrow. The important thing is to not stop questioning." – Albert Einstein

"Let your hopes, not your hurts, shape your future." – Robert H. Schuller

"Hope is being able to see that there is light despite all the darkness." – Desmond Tutu

IDENTITY

Some of life's biggest questions…. Who am I? Why am I here? And What am I capable of doing? It seems normal that every person would have at some point asked themselves these things? While there is a very complicated scientific and psychology based explanation as to how identities are formed, I am going to keep it quite simple. Your identify is defined as the characteristics of self that determines how you see yourself, or how you think that others see you. A child's identity is altered and formed over years by hundreds of experiences, interactions with others, and their own unique, innate personality.

It took years for you to come up with what you think about yourself. While identity forming starts almost at birth, the real identity formation comes when we get a little older, and are trying to figure out what sets us apart from other people. Yes, it can be race, culture, hair color, eye color, sense of style. But it goes deeper than that. It is what we believe of ourselves, and how we think the rest of the world sees us. Examples of identity traits that we relate to are happy, sad, fat, skinny, helpful, confident, bashful, intelligent or stupid. It's how we feel inside.

Where does this identity come from? How is it formed? It comes from the people around us. It starts with our parents, grandparents, siblings and caregivers. Then at school age it progresses to people in the church, teachers, sports coaches, and every other person we spend any significant amount of time with. We take little bits and pieces of every single interaction and what we see other people saying we are, and we believe it. Again, that is the very most simplistic information, but it is important to see a glimpse at why you may feel at times that the person you see in the mirror is not the person that you think you are.

Let's look at two different scenarios.... Scenario one... You grow up in a loving and supportive family environment. From day one the people that you are around give you "Facts" about yourself that you hear. "You are such a beautiful child", "You are going to do amazing things", "You are so precious" "I love you", "I can't wait to see what a super human being you grow up to be". That is scenario one. So what identity do you adopt? You feel beautiful, precious, loved, super, amazing. What other people tell you, you have ingrained into your psyche. After hearing it enough, you believe it, and IDENTIFY with it.

Now take a different scenario. Your mom drinks, your dad drinks. Your home is stressful and violent and changing every single moment. What are you told at a very young age? "You're chubbier than the other kids at school", "You don't do anything right", "You make life so stressful. I wish you were never born." "Having you around is such a pain. I don't have time to do all the stuff you want to do." Or even worse, a backhanded compliment, which I am sure you are familiar with. "I know you're smart, I wish you would use your brain to do something worthwhile." So how does this person feel? What does he/she identify as? Fat, unable to do anything right, in the way, not worthy of love, unwanted, and unmotivated.

Is it starting to make a little sense? Now I want to do a small exercise. You don't have to share it with anyone. It is just for you. I want you to write down ten different traits that you feel describe you the best, the words that you identify with the best. Now, I want you to put yourself in someone else's shoes. Someone you get along with. Someone you think really likes you. This could be your best friend, your sibling who you love to death, an aunt or uncle, or a teacher who you really respect. Now write down ten traits that you think that person would say you had.

Do you have your list? Now Cross ANYTHING off of the two lists that is negative. I want you to only keep positive words on the paper! If it even seems remotely negative, cross it off so hard you can't even read it.

Now on a clean piece of paper, write "I AM "Now write down just the positive words that you have on that first piece of paper. Your paper should now look something like this:

I AM:
Kind
Understanding
Friendly
Helpful
Smart
Loving
Wise
Trustworthy
YOU NOW HAVE YOUR "I AM" LIST

Read this list every day, if not several times a day. After about a month, I assure you that you will start to feel better about yourself. Not only will you be able to hear a compliment about yourself and not dismiss it, but you will be able to better dismiss anything negative that is thrown your way. When you know in your heart you are amazing and good, NOBODY will be able to tell you differently.

JOY

Dictionary.com defines joy in this way: the emotion of great delight or happiness caused by something exceptionally good or satisfying.

Christian joy is a good feeling in the soul, produced by the Holy Spirit, as he causes us to see the beauty of Christ in the world.vi

Either way, you may be thinking, how do I get some? Where do I find it in my life? All I feel in my soul is fear, frustration, sadness, despair, confusion and dread for my future.

I get it. Joy, happiness, serenity, and peace seem to you at this moment just a pipe dream, and something that you can never truly experience. I know you CAN experience true joy, and I am going to help get you there. While you practice these methods, however, I want to make sure that you first understand the difference between happiness and joy. While happiness is an emotion where you are feeling great, it is external. Happiness can be felt on somewhat of a superficial level. You are happy that you got your new pair of shoes. You are happy that mom isn't coming home tonight and you can get some sleep. You are happy that your job gave you the day off so that you could study for your test. Those are examples of happiness, which are extremely enjoyable, but it is a temporary feeling that is dependent on external experiences. True joy is an inner feeling. It endures trials, tribulations and endures hardships. True joy is an inner feeling that encompasses comfort, peace and pure bliss. It is most definitely an attitude of your heart and your spirit, and it a **choice** that we must consciously make on a daily basis.

So I can choose to be joyful when my whole life is falling apart? How? In many of the same ways that we choose to practice gratitude. Just a few tips:

- Smile more
- Exercise
- Practice Gratitude
- Take a deep breath
- Stay well rested
- Eat well
- Give someone less fortunate than you a compliment
- Be in the present, pay attention to the moment
- Celebrate small wins
- Spend time alone, and "just listen"
- Stop worrying about what might happen
- Laugh
- Read your "I am" list and feel good about yourself

KNOWLEDGE

Have you ever heard the expression "Knowledge is power"? If you are here right now, you are probably seeking knowledge. And you definitely know you could use some POWER in this situation. While this book discusses quite a few topics, we do not go into depth into any of them. As I mentioned, each topic we discuss could be a book in itself. My hope for you is that this book makes you want to learn more. There are so many different places to go for more information. On page 84 of the book is a list of resources and some of my favorite books to read. However, there are more than just books. Below is a short list of the places you can go for more information, and you can pick the method that works best for you. What's important is that you learn as much about the disease and how to deal with it as you can. There is a gold mine of information at your fingertips to help you become more equipped to deal with your alcoholic, your home life, and ultimately your future! Take advantage of it. You won't be sorry.

1. Al-anon Family Groups: http://al-anon.org/
2. ChildHelp USA Child Abuse Hotline: 1-800-422-4453
3. Books (List of favorites on page 84
4. Google

5. Face Book Groups – (Children of Alcoholics Thriving Now) is my Page
6. NACOA – National Association of Children of Addiction – a great resource

While this list is not exhaustive, it is a great place to start. Arm yourself with as much knowledge of the disease and its affects as you can. I have mentioned several times that there was going to be quite a bit of work for you to do to get to where you want to be, but I promise you will not be disappointed. As al-anon says "work the program because the program works" Education is always a great place to start.

LAUNDRY LIST

In 1978, the Co-founder of Adult Children of Alcoholics (ACA) came up with a list of 14 traits that children raised in dysfunctional families often possessed as adults. He called it the laundry list . For this section I am simply going to list them, and then we can take a moment to reflect. These are in no way a list of traits you WILL have, just a list of what could potentially happen to you if you go through your teens and young adulthood without getting the help, support and tools that you desperately need. That is the object of this book, 100%. So often therapy and self-help starts when we are adults. If you scour the internet, you find hundreds of books on ADULT children of alcoholics.

Well, my hope for you and everyone else that reads or shares this book is that teens start the healing process NOW, before they are adults, and much of the damage is done. I like to call it my own little version of Soul Band-Aids that do the job before the wounds scar. So take a look at this list of things that COULD happen, take a minute and reflect and then change your mindset. Decide RIGHT NOW that you will be conscious enough of the list to want to learn the skills to be able to combat this list, one item at a time.

LAUNDRY LIST

1. We become isolated and afraid of people and authority figures
2. We became approval seekers and lost our identity in the process
3. We are frightened by angry people and any personal criticism
4. We either become alcoholics, marry them or both, or find another compulsive
   personality such as a workaholic to fulfill our sick abandonment needs
5. We live life from the viewpoint of victims and we are attracted by that
   weakness in our love and friendship relationships
6. We have an overdeveloped sense of responsibility and it is easier to be
   concerned with others rather than ourselves. This enables us not to look
   too closely at our own faults, etc
7. We get guilt feelings when we stand up for ourselves instead of giving in to
   others
8. We become addicted to excitement
9. We confuse love and pity and tend to "love" people we can "pity" and "rescue"
10. We have stuffed our feelings from our traumatic childhoods and have lost
    the ability to feel or express our feelings because it hurts so much
11. We judge ourselves harshly and have a very low sense of self-esteem
12. We are dependent personalities who are terrified of abandonment and will
    do anything to hold on to a relationship in order not to experience painful
    abandonment feelings, which we received from living with sick people who
    were never there emotionally for us
13. We became para-alcoholics and took on the characteristics of that disease
    even thought we did not pick up a drink
14. We are reactors rather that actors, or proactors
    (A., Tony, 1978, https://adultchilren.org)

MANIPULATION

Are you tired of being completely manipulated by your alcoholic? Do you feel as though they lie, deny, make up, spin the truth, or do anything else that they have to do to get you to see it their way? If so, you are not alone. Manipulation is a huge part of an addicts life for many reasons. To understand the basics of why addicts manipulate so regularly, we must be reminded of the fact that alcoholism is a disease. This disease actually changes the brain, and the way it works and thinks. While a non-alcoholic derives pleasure from things such as love, friendships, exercise, enjoying the outdoors, or even a good meal, that is not the case for the alcoholic. An alcoholic gets a sense of instant gratification from the feel good effects of alcohol. This instant gratification is much stronger than the satisfaction that they get from what we would consider "Normal Pleasures". Because of that, not only do they need more and more of the feeling, but because there is a change in "normal" logical thinking, the consequences and judgement calls during this "Fix" go right out the window. While we might stop something pleasurable, such as a nice walk in the park, because we know it is time for us to go to work, the alcoholic does not care. The gratification of the alcohol makes them continue to seek more.

Even when the idea of negative consequences arise, the need to continue drinking wins out. When this happens, the alcoholic is left feeling embarrassed, ashamed, wronged, guilty and sad. It is a vicious cycle that perpetuates itself over and over again. To kill those feelings the alcoholic manipulates everyone around them to avoid dealing with the truth of what is really happening.

While there are many different types of manipulation used by alcoholics, four major ones will be discussed. . These seem to be the ones that I saw so often as a child, and the ones that I talk to children about almost every day when they open up and share the things that go on in their lives. If it happens to the majority of children of alcoholics that I talk to, I can probably assume that it happens to you or the person that you care about that brought you this far into the book.

The first form of manipulation is called gas lighting. The term actually came from a play written and performed back in 1938. It was a film about a man who convinced a woman that she was crazy by manipulating what really happened and what he told her happened. He did this so that he could gain her inheritance. He did it so well and was so manipulating that she ended up being committed to a mental institution, and his plan worked.

Since then it has become a very common practice in psychological abuse. It happens a lot with alcoholics and other addicts. It is a way of controlling the person by making them question their own sanity. When they question their own sanity, not only do they lose their self confidence and self esteem, but they also become more emotionally dependent on the addict because they doubt that they have the mental capacity to do anything without that person.

I remember very distinctly an episode in which this was done to me. I was in the sixth grade. I arrived home from school one day only to find that my mother had rearranged all the books on my bookshelf, going from tallest to shortest. I am not sure why she did it to this day, but I know for sure that I didn't do it. When I questioned it, she told me that she sat and watched me do it, and "I was crazy if I didn't remember moving the books". This happened several days in a row where she would move something or take something and then blame me. After several days, for just a split moment, I remember thinking that maybe I had done it, and didn't even realize I had done it. My father told me in no uncertain circumstances that he saw her do it, but I still questioned it while I lay in bed at night. Was I crazy? Did I do something and not even remember it? Could I have been that distraught that I literally blacked out doing something that made me appear so neurotic? It took me awhile, but I eventually learned to not question myself as much as I questioned her. Unfortunately, however, I still question myself on a regular basis when my thinking does not agree with someone else's, or we have conflicting memories of past events. It takes a long time to retrain your brain to trust yourself, but it can be done.

The second form of manipulation that is used a lot is the "Overly nice syndrome". That is when the alcoholic is soooo nice that you feel bad for having been angry with them. How could you possibly be mad at someone when they treated you so well? The guilt it causes makes the child of an alcoholic not only feel guilty, but also acquire a false sense of hope in thinking that things will get better and the abuse and drunken behavior will end. Of course this is short lived, but it works to make the child feel bad for just a minute. It also gives the alcoholic a chance to let go of their own guilt if even just for a short time.

Another form of manipulation is blame shifting. Of course, nothing is ever the alcoholics fault. If they are arrested, it is the policeman's fault for stopping them when they were doing nothing wrong. If they are caught stealing it is dad's fault for not having money in the account when it is needed. If there is a scene at the school, it is your fault for having to get involved and making her do all these stupid things after all. Does any of this ring a bell? Shifting blame is convenient, and an easy way to take the blame off of the alcoholic for awhile. Unfortunately, it is emotionally exhausting for the person (Yourself a lot of the time) for getting blamed.

The final manipulation tactic that I will mention is the guilt tripping. This is a huge one and one which I would be amazed if you or any child of an active alcoholic has ever escaped. Guilt tripping is a manipulation technique in which a person makes you feel bad enough about something that you change how you act, or what you do; many times against your better judgement. An alcoholic parent will do this so that the attention is taken off of them and put onto you. Now the focus is on you and what you did or did not do, and not them. It is incredibly manipulative, and so bad for our self worth if we let it continue.

Has a conversation with your unruly alcoholic ever sounded like this…

"If you loved me you would get me another bottle"

"After all the things I have done for you and you won't even give me a ride"

"Fine, I will drive, but if I get in an accident and die it will be nobody's fault but yours. Can you live with that?"

"You always take your fathers side. I bet you wish I wasn't even around."

While statements like that are hurtful and meant to cause that guilty feeling, you don't have to submit to the guilt. There are a number of different things that you can do to get rid of the guilty feeling. Ironically, they all include taking care of your own mental well being, and not worrying about what the alcoholic is saying. You know in your mind that they are just saying it to hurt you, so DO NOT LET IT! The key to surviving this passive/ aggressive form of manipulation is communication and boundaries.

- Let them know how you feel about them trying to make you feel guilty. Voice out loud that it will not work
- Recognize that this form of manipulation is because they are emotionally immature, not you. You be the bigger person and ignore the best you can what they have said
- Do self -talk and positive affirmations to reassure yourself that what they said is not true.
- Face the guilt trip directly, and deal with it. If there is no merit in it, dismiss it as just another drunken rant
- Set boundaries. If you are being guilted into doing something that you know is wrong, stand your ground. Refuse to do something that you know is wrong and tell them why
- Do not give them the satisfaction of a response. Sometimes not saying anything, or saying a quick "I am sorry that you feel that way, but I don't agree" comment can be enough. You have had your say, letting them know that you will not feel badly, or change what you do for anything

- When all else fails, get out of the situation as quickly as possible. Sometimes in the heat of the moment, your alcoholic is saying anything they can to make you feel badly. You know you can't reason with them, and you do not want to make the situation more volatile than it already is. Just remove yourself entirely from the situation.

While all four types of manipulation are detrimental to the well being and the mental health of the person on the receiving end, it does not have to be that way. Learn to identify when you are being manipulated, set firm boundaries, and continue working on being the you that you want to be. Remember, the whole premise of this book is to stop being hyper focused on the actions and attitudes of the alcoholic, and invest your time and energy into working on you. This is a perfect example of a time when you should do that.

NORMALCY

While there is really no such things as a "Normal" household, there is definitely not one in a home with an alcoholic. Even if there was, you would probably not recognize normal anyway.

Jane remembered her childhood saying: "My home was always filled with so much chaos. Fights broke out on a regular basis for no reason. There was never any consistency. I lived in fear of what was happening and in dread of what was to come. I would often retreat to my best friends house for entire weeks, just so I could experience what I thought could be considered normal. My parents never even knew I was gone."

It was actually a good idea, her going to a friends house. It is important that you put yourself in situations whenever possible to experience different ideas of "normal". Staying in your own toxic environment all the time has to be incredibly draining on you, I can only imagine. Get out. Be a teenager. This is your time to enjoy and you deserve to have some fun. Join clubs or groups. Sign up for activities that you are interested in. Sometimes it is enough just to get out of the house for a few hours a day, or even a few hours a week. You deserve to be a normal teen, doing normal things that normal teens do. Just a few times a week outside of the chaos of your home is enough for you to take a breather, relax and enjoy the "other side". Choose now to make a life outside of your chaotic mess of a home and do the things that "Normal" people do. But remember, there is no right "normal". You have to experience different experiences and situations in order to be able to decide for yourself what you think is normal.

NEGLECT

While we touched on neglect when we were discussing abuse, I want to take just a minute and talk a little bit more about neglect. I am not sure why, but it seems like such a silent form of abuse, that I want to make sure that you still understand the impact it can have. What exactly is neglect? Basically it is when a parent or caregiver fails to give proper attention or satisfy basic needs. When you think of neglect, what do you picture? A dog locked up outside in the heat crouching in the corner, filthy, emaciated, and looking absolutely starved of every basic necessity life should afford him/her? Well, the neglect that a child of an alcoholic sometimes faces is no different. It is a slow and debilitating form of abuse that takes its toll in a short amount of time. But the toll is so deeply ingrained into our psyche, that it is hard to come back from.

When we discussed the four types of abuse, which do you imagine would be the most common? If I had to guess, I would have said 1- Physical 2- Emotional 3- Neglect and then 4-Sexual. That would have been my first instinct. Boy, would I have been wrong. In an article last published on June 14, 2022, taking into consideration just physical, sexual and neglect, the results were staggering. They stated that of known cases of abuse, 9% were sexually abused, 18% were physically abused and a staggering 78% were victims of severe neglect! [viii] Then why, I can't help but wonder, is it so seldom on the forefront of the news, or the main focus of dysfunctional family dynamics? Probably because it is less in our faces. Unless we see a child going through the garbage or coming to school with no shoes, we do not always see that neglect is even occurring. There are also more than just the neglect that we can see. When talking about child neglect specifically, there are four main types of neglect. Listen to the descriptions of these and see if you or the person you are reading this book for fit into any of these categories.

1. Physical Neglect: The failure to provide basic physical needs, such as food, clothing, shelter, and supervision
2. Emotional Neglect: The failure to meet a child's emotional needs or psychosocial support
3. Educational Neglect: The failure to send a child to school or provide the proper educational needs
4. Medical Neglect: The failure to provide a child with proper medical or mental health treatment.

Do any of those sound familiar? Can you imagine the damage that any one of these can do to you? I would like to focus for just a minute on the emotional neglect, since I believe that that is the one that is less visible and often goes unnoticed.

Teachers, friends, clergy, counselors and coaches are around children out of the home. However, they do not see what happens in the home. They can not see if a child is getting proper love and attention. Unfortunately, by the time a child starts to show the effects of emotional neglect, their brains have already changed to adapt.

Emotional neglect is a form of psychological maltreatment, or abuse. It can be just as damaging and physical abuse, and is usually much more damaging than sexual abuse. Again, I am simply touching on this topic, as it could be a whole book in itself. (Simon Chapple wrote a very good book I recommend called "How to Heal Your Inner Child: Overcome Past Trauma and Childhood Emotional Neglect"

When a child is emotionally neglected their needs for love, support, affection, security and teaching are not being met. Not just once or twice, as no parent is perfect, but on a continual basis. When a child continually reaches our for this emotional support, only to be pushed away or ignored, it can have detrimental effects on their psychological development. It is the same as when a child cries or is hurt and they are met with "Don't cry, or I'll give you something to cry about." You remember those words, right? Being dismissed over and over makes a child feel as though his or her emotions don't count, are not valid, or just wrongin general. Years of this can lead to a distorted emotional intelligence and all sorts of problems down the road.

What happens to children that have been emotionally neglected? They often suffer signs of trauma such as PTSD. They shut down and refuse to ask for help with anything. They suffer physical ongoing symptoms such as headaches and stomach aches. They have a really hard time making friends and keeping them. They do not trust anybody, and have a hard time maintaining relationships. They can not deal with emotions; theirs or someone else's. They also suffer an immense amount of anxiety, depression, mood disorders and mental illness later in life. Sounds terrible, yes, but can you be helped if you have suffered from emotional neglect?

Of course you can. The first thing is to identify if you have been a victim of emotional neglect. Ask yourself a few questions.

1. Did your parents show you affection when you were younger? A hug, a kiss, an "I Love You"
2. When you cried were they supportive, or were you told to "SUCK IT UP" or something to that effect
3. When you were scared did they comfort you or send you back to your room to deal with it?
4. Were you ridiculed a lot and called names such as "Pansy" "Wussy girl or boy" "Baby" "Crybaby" or other names when you were having a tough time?
5. Did you frequently observe inappropriate behavior in your home and then told to keep it quiet?
6. Were there violent fights or circumstances in which you were afraid, but not allowed to talk about?
7. Were you kept from people that you loved, such as a grandparent or friend?
8. Were you allowed or encouraged to drink alcohol with your parents at a very young age?
9. When you tried to ask for your parents help were you told to "Go away" or "Leave them alone" even when it seemed important to you?
10. Were you constantly ridiculed or made fun of by your parent/caregiver?

If you said "Yes' to any of these, and especially if it happened more than once, you most likely have been emotionally neglected. But don't worry. Now you know, you can get help.

By now you are probably sick to death of hearing me say that you need to get help. However, that is what this book is all about.

It is all about getting you to the resources and support that you need to get to in order to be able to emerge into adulthood without all the baggage of your youth. You were dealt a pretty crappy hand, not by choice. But you can make a choice to change the deck of cards starting now. When I refused to go to therapy, one because I still felt too much shame and didn't think it would help and two, because I couldn't afford it, I looked for other options. I went to Alanon groups. I joined online support groups for Children of Alcoholics. I did research... tons of it. I did about anything I could to be with people, or read about people in my same situation. I figured even if I never shared one second of my story, knowing I had a support group out there for me was enough. I was right and I was wrong. It started as enough. I made tons of friends who gave me the love and support that I needed. I finally had a group of people who understood. Then it was time to share my story. Once I opened up and told people what really happened, an amazing thing happened.... I started believing everything that I heard, and I started to heal. I encourage you to do the same. Join groups, go to Alateen meetings, do research. I have included a list of really good books out there for you to read, but just scouring the internet a few minutes a day will give you so much knowledge. And knowledge is power, as I have mentioned. No, I take that back. Knowledge is POTENTIAL POWER. You can have all the knowledge in the world, but if you don't do anything with it, it is useless. So, as your emotionally neglectful parent may have said to you, "Pull up your big girl/boy pants and get it done", I am saying it to you.. But with love and a true desire to watch you get it done.

OVERACHIEVER

You want everything in your world to be perfect, right? You want straight A's, you want to look your best, be your best, do everything the best. If you are on a sports team, you strive to be captain. If you are in a book club, you strive to read more books than anyone else. If you are getting ready to be in a spelling contest, you study until you make yourself go crazy. Sound familiar? Ever wonder why? It is called the overachiever syndrome. It is one of the family roles that children of alcoholics adapt to, and one very much worth mentioning. I'll talk a little bit about it, but I want to make one very thing abundantly clear right from the beginning. You do not have to be perfect. Being perfect is not going to help your alcoholic want to stop drinking. Being perfect is not going to take the attention off of the poor behavior of your alcoholic and divert it to you. You deserve to let go of that burden you have put on yourself, and just be a kid!

I remember coming home with a report card in which I got all A's and one B. It was 8th grade. It had been a really sad year and I had struggled really hard to get anything at all done at home. I got myself involved in every activity I could possibly think of to keep me out of the house, and even worked two part time jobs. Mom was finally getting ready to move out, and although it seemed like it should be a happy time, it was not. I was under constant stress. The fighting in my house had hit an all time high. There were fights between my mother and father, fights between my mother and brother, fights between my father and brother (usually trying to keep one of them from hurting my mother when things got too bad).

Fights between all of us. Several times the police had been to the house for domestic calls and my level of anxiety was off the charts.

I look back now, and realize what I thought was just heartburn so bad it made me vomit, was actually me having full blown anxiety attacks. I figured I would also be diagnosed with asthma if I went to the doctor, since when I was having my "Episodes", I could barely breathe.

Anyway, back to the report card…. That report card was the highlight of my day. No, let me rephrase that… Bringing home that report card was the highlight of my year. I was, for just a brief moment, proud of my accomplishments, and proud of the fact that I could push through and be able to focus enough to actually be productive. That moment was soooo brief. I went to show it to my mom, she was too drunk to even look at it. She told me to "go show it to your perfect father. I don't give a shit. He'll appreciate it though". I showed it to my dad, who I absolutely adored and respected so much. His reaction was shocking as well. "It's about time you use the brain God gave you. Let's see how long that lasts." Wow! I didn't see that coming. A quarter of a year, and all that work, and I felt smaller and more insignificant than I could ever remember. I really let it get to me. I shouldn't have. I should have remained proud of my accomplishments and ignored what people said about me. I regret that now. The next marking period I did it again, but I never showed anyone those report cards again. I also never felt good about my grades again.

PARENTING

Parenting is something that we all take for granted. Unfortunately, we don't get to choose our parents. And if you're reading this book today, your parents are probably ones that you would not have chosen for yourself. Often, when you live with the instability of one or both of your parents being alcoholics, you become the parent. Unfortunately, this happens when you are just a child yourself, and really need a parent to lean on. Think about when you started taking on the role of a parent? Do you remember cooking , cleaning, or caring for yourself and possibly siblings while all your other friends were out doing "KID" things? I don't know how many times I can remember tucking my mom in to bed, or cleaning up the vomit on the bathroom floor so nobody slipped and got hurt. At 8 years old, I was doing a lot of the cooking and cleaning, with the help of my older brother. I can even remember making sure that my dad had clean clothes for work the next day, knowing that both mom and dad would be passed out and drunk before it could get done. A lack of parentel support makes you lose those years of childhood and throws you into roles you are not ready for .

Well, you can't change your parents. You don't get to choose different ones, ones that are going to care for you and feed you and take you fun places. But you can try to put yourself in situations where you are around nurturing and loving parents. When you choose your friends, it is going to be a natural tendency to choose children that are in the same situation as you. I had a best friend since Kindergarten, and our parents drank together. All the time. While at the time it seemed comfortable, knowing that they were not going to shame me or embarrass me by their drunk behavior, if I could do it over again, I would do it differently. I would choose friends whose parents didn't drink. Friends whose parents I could sit down and talk to. Friends whose parents would make me feel safe and secure for those few hours when I could escape from the harsh realties of my own parents. I encourage you to try to have a variety of friends, and to visit them often. I am not saying not to love your parents... I am not saying that at all. I just want to encourage you to seek out what every child deserves, and that is some sense of stability. There is a good book that I suggest called "When Your Parent Drinks Too Much". It reiterates a lot of what I am saying, just a different perspective.

Parenting is hard enough when you don't struggle with a number of other issues. Unfortunately, your parents are dealing with the issue of alcoholism. I say parents, because even if only one is an alcoholic, the other deals with it themselves, on so many different levels. Often times, the non drinking parent is just as incapable of giving you what you need because they have to deal with the drinking spouse. It is a battle for everyone in the family, as we mentioned. Everyone has to deal with it their own way. All you can do is take care of yourself, and that is the number one goal of this book. It's not about the parents, the alcoholics,or the other people in your life affected by this disease. It is about you!

QUESTIONS

By now you probably have gotten some answers, but you may also be swimming with questions…. Great ! That means you want to learn. Please never stop having questions. Here I am going to just put a few of the most asked questions that I have gotten during my times teaching and speaking to children in your situation. If you have other questions that are not answered, please feel free to go to my website at www.tammyvincent.com or my Facebook page "children of alcoholics thriving now" and reach out to me directly. Remember that both sites are 100% confidential, and NO QUESTION is too silly to ask. If you have the question, there are probably several people out there in your situation that have the same question. You having the courage to ask could help hundreds or even thousands of people. Isn't it nice to see how us all working together can change so many lives for the better?

❖ Is there anything that I can do to help my alcoholic quit drinking?

    – No, there is nothing that you can do. Your alcoholic has to want to quit. What you can do is use as many techniques in this book that are offered to try to take the best care of yourself that you can.

❖ My intoxicated parent is always trying to get me to get in the car when they have been drinking. Is there another option? What would you do?

    – Your own safety and the safety of the people close to you such as a younger sibling is your number one priority. You can refuse and say that you do not want to go. Come up with as many excuses as possible. If they get violent , or cause you harm, this is one situation in which I would say it is ok to call the authorities on them. While it may seem horrible at the time, sometimes that is the wake up call that they need to make them understand the problem that they face. Regardless, it is NEVER ok to let an intoxicated parent put you in physical harm.

❖ My mom doesn't hurt me physically , but is super mean and hardly ever feeds me. I know some people have it so much worse and I should not feel sorry for myself, but when she drinks things are so bad. Am I wrong to be upset?

    – Absolutely not! Abuse and trauma and neglect come in so many different forms. Just because you are not physically hurt, short of being hungry, ABUSE AND

NEGLECT are still detrimental to your psyche, your self esteem and your development as a young adult. Please know that there is nothing wrong with seeking help, and we encourage you to do that.

- ❖ My mom gets drunk and says and does horrible things. The next morning she says that she does not remember. Is this possible?

  – Yes, this is called an alcoholic blackout and that memory is never actually formed. When they tell you that they do not remember, they are telling the truth. I explain blackouts in more detail back in the section about Blackouts.

- ❖ Why can't my alcoholic parent stop drinking? It seems like if they loved me enough, they would stop for me.

  – Alcoholism is a disease, just as cancer is a disease. The main characteristic of alcoholism is that the drinker is unable to stop when they want, and it has detrimental effects on the family. An alcoholic has a physiological need for alcohol that is just as strong as a diabetic has a need for insulin.

- ❖ What are the chances that my alcoholic parent will stop drinking? Will this go on forever?

  – The percentage of alcoholics that go into recovery is about 36%, as of 2021. The percentage of those that continue to abstain from drinking is approximately 33%. With that being said you can hopefully see the importance of taking this time to not focus 100% on fixing them, but rather helping yourself to learn to better cope, deal and heal yourself.

❖ What causes an alcoholic to drink?

   – There is no one specific activity or event that causes all alcoholics to start drinking. That we know for sure. However, what we do know is that the drinking continues in an effort to suppress negative emotions, numb the pain of past traumas, or just to forget sadness. We also know that the more an alcoholic drinks, the less they will be able to control themselves in the future, and the more they will become physically dependent on the alcohol to get through life. We also know that alcohol withdrawal is one of the hardest withdrawals to go through, and can lead to serious health consequences and even death.

❖ If my parents are alcoholics does that mean that I am going to become an alcoholic?

   – There is no proof that just because your parents are alcoholics that you will become one. There are genes that are linked to addictive tendencies, and alcoholism does tend to run in families. Research is not 100% certain, however, that these generational illnesses do not stem more from a social and situational cause as to a genetic cause. However, since you are aware that alcoholism runs in your family (especially if it goes back several generations), it is worth it to be cautious and make mindful decisions about alcohol when the time comes. I felt that I had definitely inherited my parents addictive tendencies, but chose for alcohol not to be my "Pain reliever" so to speak.

❖ I have heard that children of alcoholics will grow up to have so many different problems because of how they were raised, and the way they were treated. Is this true?

    – NO, not true. It can be true, but that is why we are here. You have the power to decide right now that you will empower yourself to learn about this disease, and help yourself starting right now. You have so many resources available to you. You just have to decide that you want to put in the work. I encourage everyone reading this to begin NOW to become the person you want to be. Alcoholism is very often generational, passing down tendencies and inherited traits and characteristics from one generation to the next. My own personal family goes at least four generations deep with alcoholism on both my parents side of the family. But it won't get me! I made the CONSCIOUS choice that I was not going to be my parents, or my grandparents, or my great-grand parents, or their.....

NOPE! My brother, sister and I are all choosing t break the cycle right now!

RESOURCES

This is a sample list of some resources that I think you may enjoy. This is not a complete list, but just a place to start.

- After the Tears – By Lorie Dwinell
- Courage To Change: One Day at a Time in Al-Anon – By Al-anon Family Groups
- How to Heal Your Inner Child: Overcome Past Trauma and Childhood Emotional Neglect – Simon Chapple
- It Will Never Happen To Me – By Claudia Black
- Perfect Daughters. Adult Daughters of Alcoholics – By Robert J Ackerman PHD
- 7 Things That Change Everything- By Jody Lamb
- The Deepest Well, - Healing the Long-term Effects of Childhood Adversity by Nadine Burke Harris, M.D.
- The Boy Who Was Raised As A Dog – By Bruce D Perry, MD, PHD and Maia Szalavitz
- Complex PTSD: From Surviving to Thriving: A Guide and Map for Recovering from Childhood Trauma
- Https://al-anon.org
- https://nacoa.org/families
- National Domestic Violence Hotline. That number is 800-799-SAFE

ROLE MODELS

Your parents should be your most positive and encouraging role model while you are growing up. Parents are there to foster their children's self-esteem as well as help them form a positive sense of identity. Unfortunately, however, often when there is one or more alcoholic parents in the family, these role models are non-existent and children are forced to grow up taking guesses at what is normal, and learning the best they can.

Luckily, there are other people in your life that can serve as that positive role model. Our hope is that we steer you in the direction of that person and you allow them to help you in learning a little bit more of a sense of "normalcy", even though there is really no such thing as normal.

Think about who you have in your life that you admire, like, respect, and look up to. It could be a special teacher, a counselor, an aunt, uncle, coach, youth group leader, or anyone else that you are around. Now that you have that person, let me ask you something…. Would they be shocked to know that you are going through a horrible time in your life right now? You've spent your whole life just trying to survive, all on your own. At this point you probably feel unworthy of the attention, undeserving of the love, and not good enough to have the time wasted on you! Again, I am going to get up in your face and call

BS! You are an amazing person who just got dealt a tough hand. There's no way that God just decided he didn't want to make you great! That doesn't happen. He makes everyone great! You deserve to be treated as such. I encourage you to seek help from one of the people that you thought of when I first mentioned people that you admire. I can assure you that if you think that they are good, they will be more than happy to help you out. You just have to put yourself out there. I know it may be uncomfortable, It may be one of the hardest things you ever have to do in your life. Admitting you need help is not something to be ashamed of. Wanting to have a better life is not something to be ashamed of. And telling someone that your parents are not there for you, and you need someone in your corner, is MOST CERTAINLY not something to be ashamed of.

I challenge you that if you have not talked to anyone about what is going on in your life up to this point, that you DO IT NOW! It is never too early to start taking care of yourself, and you will be absolutely amazed at the support and encouragement you will get from people if you just ask.

I didn't ask. I didn't tell. I didn't show. I didn't share. I didn't cry. I didn't yell. I kept silent, and suffered for years. I suffered feelings of loss, fear, heartache, pain, torture, abuse, humiliation and shame all by myself. I started reaching out in my early thirties, when a lot of the damage was already done. I now have a sponsor, a mentor, a best friend, a confidante, and a sense of self. Don't wait another minute. Go get help now. You deserve to be loved and there are people out there that would love to help.

SAFETY

When it comes to keeping yourself and the people you love safe around your alcoholic, this is NOT NEGOTIABLE. This may include yourself, other siblings, friends, and often times the sober parent. There are so many volatile and unsafe situations that arise when a person has lost control because of drinking. It may be your alcoholic's drinking and driving, non-controlled violent moods, or just in general the crazy drunken rants that an alcoholic goes through when they have had too much to drink. You should always have a plan, and be aware of your surroundings. If you drive, it may mean hiding a spare set of keys where only you know where they are so you can leave at any time, or being ready at a moments notice to be ready to flee the house. It may involve having a friend who will be there if you need them. It may involve calling the police. Either way, it will involve you being hypervigilant to what is going on around you, and ready to be on the defensive at the drop of a dime. Hopefully after finishing this book, you will be able to remember during these unsafe times that it is still ok to breathe.

Do you remember a time or even multiple times when you felt that your safety was at risk? Were there times when your alcoholic tried to get you to get in a car with them when they had been drinking, or when there were fights in your house that got so violent, you felt the need to flee?? It is your right to be safe. Even if it means calling 9-1-1- and having them show up at the house.

Unfortunately, even if it means having your parent arrested. Right now it may seem too embarrassing or shameful to admit that things have really gotten that bad, but the reality of it is that if you are not safe, and you are in a situation of being badly injured , or God forbid, fatally injured, you owe it to yourself to try to take care of yourself.

You are probably aware by now that so many of your circumstances put you in a situation where you literally were just trying to make it through the day. I commend you for having the tenacity and coping skills to get this far. Now I want you to understand that it is your God given right to feel safe. Parents are supposed to do that for you, but if they do not, you need to do whatever you can to maintain that safety.

If you are in a life-threatening or very dangerous situation, you can always call 9-1-1. If you want you can also call the National Domestic Violence Hotline. That number is 800-799-SAFE. It may seem terrifying at the time, but things can escalate quickly to a very dangerous situation, and you do not want yourself or anyone else in that type of situation.

I went through six months of my life where I felt completely unsafe almost all the time. I kick myself now for not having the faith in the people and system around me to tell anybody what was happening. My father and step-mother (who ironically was my mothers' best friend before they got married) kicked me out of the house to go live with my mother. It was without a doubt, the scariest time of my life. I moved from my hometown in New Jersey to a tiny little house in the middle of the woods in Sudbury, Massachusetts. The nearest store was miles away and I felt like I was on an island all by myself. My mom lived in a little room off of my Aunt Judy's garage. I slept on a dingy couch, with little or no food to eat for several months. It was horrible. I'm embarrassed to say it, but it was a time in which I not only tried to end my own life, but also planned in my head over and over how I could end hers. (God forgive me).

The orange juice, if there was any, was always a mixture of ½ juice and ½ vodka. There was never any food to eat, and my mom was so deep into her addiction that she would go weeks without going to the grocery store. But I survived.

Every day at lunch I would run about a mile and a half to the grocery store. It took me about 10 minutes to get there and 10 minutes to get back. That left me exactly 20 minutes to go into the store and eat as much as I could out of the packages before I had to be back at school. If they had ever called my mom and told her what I was doing, she would have been furious and the beating I would have gotten would have been terrible. Anyway, I would eat grapes out of the packages, and nuts from the dispensers. I would rip open bags of cookies and put as many as I could in my pocket. I would also steal my moms joints from her while she was sleeping, and sell them for $5.00 a piece at school. That kept me "safe" for the times when there was too much snow to get to the grocery store. I would get as much as I could possibly get at the school cafeteria, and took the rest home in my backpack, praying that she didn't find it and take it from me.

That same time my mother was "dating" a drug addict. I say dating because she spent a lot of time there. Oh, to be so young

102

and naïve again. I know they weren't dating. He was giving her free drugs in exchange for whatever sexual favors he needed from her. I can still smell his house. It smelled clean, unlike my moms house. I could smell the leather of the furniture and cigars in the ashtrays. At first I didn't mind going there because it was warm and there was always food in the fridge. Once they would pass out after their drinking and drugging binge, I would raid that fridge and eat like it was the last time I would ever eat again. Those nights I slept well, and felt "Safe".

I especially remember his garage. It was heated, not like the garage at our house. It was decorative, with couches scattered around, a dart board and a large pool table right in the center. But the thing that sticks out the most, almost 40 years later, is the record player in the corner. It sat on a huge stand, and in the stand were about fifteen little pull out drawers. When you opened the drawers, which I saw him do plenty of times, there were hundreds of little compartments all filled with pills of various sizes, shapes, and colors. At first I thought it was super cool, until I realized what it was. This is where he dealt his drugs out of. Men and women would show up at all hours of the day and night. They would come in, bang around for a few minutes and then leave. My mom was privileged to get those drugs whenever she wanted, but it wasn't without a price.

I remember the first time that my mothers' "Boyfriend" decided that it was ok to let me pay my mom's debt for her drugs. It was the nights when she was either sleeping, passed out , or just too angry and violent to give him what he needed. It was then that I realized exactly how unsafe my situation had become and yet I said NOTHING! I was angry, ashamed, and confused. I was just sixteen, had no friends , had no one to help me or love me or tell me I was worth fighting for. At that point it didn't even really matter if I was safe. I couldn't even tell my Aunt, who we lived with, for fear of her not believing me and telling my mom. I think back about it now and it makes me soooooo angry. I think back about it now and want to kick myself. I had every right to do whatever I had to do for my own safety, and I didn't do it. Those few months are a good portion of the reason that I am here today, to share with you the importance of staying safe.

There is no shame in what has happened to you. Your safety and happiness is your focus and must remain your focus! I know there are probably a thousand excuses why you think that it is ok for you to be unsafe, but I promise you, there are ZERO!

If you think that you are unsafe, there are a number of things you can do:

- Call the police
- Do not get in the car with a drunk person
- Tell teachers, counselors, anybody you trust, what is going on
- Leave the situation, get yourself out of there
- Call the National Domestic Violence Hotline. That number is 800- 799-SAFE

Basically do WHATEVER YOU HAVE TO DO to keep yourself safe. I know I have probably said this over and over, but I can not stress it enough. It is just another time where I find myself saying "If I had only known then what I know now". Well, I'm talking to you now, so you do know now!

TRAUMA

I once had a student say to me that although her parents were crazy drunk all the time, she did not have it that bad. "It's not like they hit me all the time, or show up drunk to school and embarrass me. They keep to themselves and don't really bother anybody. It could be much worse." Sound like anybody that you know? Do you downplay the severity of what is happening around you? Do you keep it a secret and think that as long as no one else is involved, it's not that big of a deal? Do you sweep the horrible things that are said and done to you under the rug because the word "abuse" "neglect" and "trauma" seem like things that only happen to other people? Well, I am here to get a little up in your face and argue that point. Trauma, abuse and neglect come in so many different forms, but they are all hard, devastating, life altering, painful and scary. And worse, if left untreated, the trauma you faced can lead to higher rates of suicide, depression, anxiety, eating disorders, PTSD, poor relationship forming and drug and alcohol use. It is not your fault that you suffered trauma, so I urge you to understand you are WORTHY of getting help.

They say that children growing up in a house with an alcoholic suffers basically the same kind of trauma that soldiers suffer when they go to war. Many Adult Children of Alcoholics (ACOA's) are treated later in life for complex PTSD, just as if they had gone to war. It is the daily, traumatic battles that a child suffers every day that leave a lasting impact on lives if they are not dealt with. Again, I know... a common theme in the book. Here I am again telling you to seek help and support, NOW, before the damage is done. Before you are looking back at a lifetime of events and facing the consequences. Before you are a different person from the happy, content, connected, well adjusted, abundantly confident person that MY GOD put you on this Earth to be.

I remember my Pre-school year. I was four years old, living in Ohio. I remember the house so vividly. There was a kitchen and living room downstairs ,and then a big open living room on it's own level (I think they called it a split level home). Then, going up the stairs, past the living room, you turned, went up five or six more stairs and to the floor with the bedrooms. Mine was the first one on the right, and the only one with neon stars decaled on the ceiling. My father had done that for me when I told him I was afraid to go to sleep and that the light of the stars helped me. A small, but quaint house, one in which I wish my father had spent more time with us. He was in the Navy at that time, and gone for months at a time. It was those months that I remembered bits and pieces of, and those months that I wish I could blank out entirely.

My mother was not working at the time. My sister was just born and mom and dad decided it would be best for my mom to stay home with us until Michelle was old enough to go to school. I had one more year, and couldn't wait to see what was out there. My brother came home happy after school and I could only imagine what he had been doing, since there was absolutely nothing at home could make me smile that big.

Every day was the same routine. Mom woke up, we watched tv and she took care of the house. Lunch time was the same EVERY DAY. She made me soft boiled eggs and toast. Sometimes the toast was burnt, sometimes it was cold, sometimes, there wasn't even any bread or toast on the plate. I never liked soft boiled eggs, and knowing now what a bad cook she was, it's no wonder. The egg whites were runny, or way overcooked. There was no perfectly done yolks like when my father made them later on. The smell of them gave me such anxiety. I knew what was coming and I knew without a doubt, it was coming at the exact same time every day.

Mom loved the show "As The World Turns". It was a popular soap opera at the time and we watched it every day while I "ate" my lunch. While it sounds like a pleasant bonding time with Michelle, Mom and I, it was anything but. I didn't like the eggs. I can say it's safe to say I disliked those eggs more than anything I had ever eaten. And I had to eat them every day. Some days I just couldn't do it. The scene was the same over and over. It started with me whining about wanting something different. "Shut up and eat your eggs or I'm going to give you something to cry about". Sound familiar? "I'll give you something to cry about" was something I heard on a regular basis, and she always kept that promise to me. When I did not eat the eggs, which sometimes took me a little while, things progressed. Sometimes I would get hit. She would spank me, put me in my room and tell me to come sit down when I was ready to eat and "Stop being so ungrateful". Sometimes she didn't even give me that chance. There was a small coat closet, right at the back of the room, right

107

next to the cat scratcher. I would be yanked by my hair, thrown in the closet, lights off and told to "Think about what happens to bad children" or something to that nature. It was so scary. I can remember the smell of the shoes, and I believe a litter box, and just nastiness in general. It was completely dark in there, and I was always afraid to move, for fear of touching something alive, dead, or unknown. Sometimes this would be over quickly, about the time that "As The World Turns" was over, or sometimes it went for hours. My big brother would come home and whenever mom wasn't looking, would lay on the floor outside of the closet and talk to me. He would even sneak me crackers and slide them under the door if he didn't think he would be caught. I wonder to this day if he remembers those days. Whether or not he does, does not matter to me. I was just grateful that he was there to keep me from being so scared.

Hours passed some days, and things got worse. If I wet myself, I got spanked. If I cried, I got spanked. If I asked to come out, I got spanked. So I just sat, sometimes for what seemed like days.

I survived that time of my life, just like I survived every other time. We moved the following year to New Jersey to be closer to my grandparents, and I started Kindergarten. I may have survived, but I never forgot. A year or so ago, I was watching tv, and from the other room, I heard the melody to "As The World Turns" on tv. Instantly, without even realizing what was happening, I vomited. My gut reaction was so strong to that melody, and the memories that it stirred up, that I instinctively just puked. Now that is what trauma does to a person. It gets ingrained so deeply into your psyche that it has ever lasting effects, and consequences that will plague you forever.

Don't ever feel that what you are going through is "Not that bad" or that "It could be worse". You deserve to have a life that doesn't included trauma, and if you've already experienced it, you deserve the opportunity to heal. Trauma takes a long time to get over. Many adult children spend years dealing with the trauma of their childhood. I encourage you, yes, again, to seek help.

I also recommend a few books that discuss dealing with childhood trauma as an adult. I've mentioned it a few times already in this book, but I feel there is so much information for ADULT CHILDREN of alcoholics and not enough for children of alcoholics. My advice is always to learn as much as you can about what you are going through so that you can begin the healing journey before some of the damage is done. I like to call it this information Soul Band-Aids, or information that works to heal the wounds BEFORE they scar.

Three books I recommend:

1. The Deepest Well, - Healing the Long-term Effects of Childhood Adversity by Nadine Burke Harris, M.D.
2. The Boy Who Was Raised As A Dog – By Bruce D Perry, MD, PHD and Maia Szalavitz
3. Complex PTSD: From Surviving to Thriving: A Guide and Map for Recovering from Childhood Trauma

UNCONDITIONAL LOVE

Is this a completely foreign concept to you? Does it even make sense? Do you relate to it, or does the concept make you chuckle? Unconditional love. It sounds pretty intense. Well, it is. It is a love, a deep love, that exists without any strings attached. It is not "I love you ..if", or "I love you.... When". It literally just means I love you. It is love that is offered freely without expecting anything in return. It is the kind of love that I get from God. I don't feel as though I have to do anything to earn it, and it just feels good. It is the kind of love that all kids deserve, and that includes you.

Do you have anyone that you feel loves you unconditionally? Do you have that kind of love for anyone? Love that no matter what they said or did to you that you could never stop loving them. Unfortunately, it is very hard to love someone unconditionally if you do not love yourself unconditionally first. I am going to go out on a limb here and say that you do not love yourself unconditionally. Am I correct?

If you have been given unconditional love from someone, embrace it. Engage with that person as much as possible and build the strongest bond you can with that person. Love them back. Even if it means learning how to do that, do it. It is an investment in yourself that you will not regret. I had one person in my life that I thought probably loved me unconditionally. It was my father's mother, my grandma. We called her "Grammes" because my older brother could not pronounce all the other versions of Grandma that were attempted, so Grammes she was. Everyone loved her. There was nothing about her not to love. She was just like a mom to me, and was always there for me. Looking back, I am pretty sure that she loved me unconditionally. Unfortunately, I was not at a point in my life that I loved myself, or trusted myself enough to share anything about my life. So, although we were extremely close, and I loved her to death, I feel that she never truly knew the real me. I never shared the things that happened to me, so I never really gave myself the chance to find out if she did indeed, love me unconditionally. It makes me so sad when I think about it. I don't want that to happen to you. I don't wish for you to be denied the feeling of unconditional love because you can't trust someone that loves you enough to fully let them in.

Unconditional love it actually something you can work on, but it takes some practice. It does not come easily, especially if you have never felt it. As I mentioned before, you can love someone unconditionally, you have to be able to have that type of love for yourself. Here are just a few ideas to try to work into your daily routine that may get you closer to being able to love yourself.

1. Focus on the positive things in your life
2. Meditate daily
3. Choose to be kind to everyone, including yourself
4. Say positive affirmations
5. Forgive yourself and try to forgive others

6. Let go of the past guilt of things you've done
7. Practice and engage in your spiritual self
8. Form and nourish relationships in which you feel loved
9. Look to see what thoughts are making you not feel lovable and examine those thoughts. See if they are real
10. Practice loving people the way that you want to be loved
11. Take care of your mental health

VICTOR OR VICTIM?

When bad things happen to us, we have a choice. We can either be sad, hurt and broken by the events, or we can rise above it, push through, and come out the other side stronger. Which way do you choose to live? I know… Seems too simple, right? Well, it is and it isn't. Choosing to remain a victim when something bad happens to you is ultimately a choice, just as choosing to be happy or choosing to be grateful is a choice. It is a CONSCIOUS choice. Don't get me wrong, I am in no way saying that what happened, or continues to happen to you is not terrible. I am not saying that you were wronged by people that you were supposed to trust, or betrayed by people that you loved. What I am saying is that if you want to move on with your life, and become happier, than you must find a way to move past it.

Exactly what is a victim mentality? A victim mentality is a persons belief that the world is out to get them, that everyone is against them and that they have no power to control any of their circumstances. Often times this sense of helplessness develops after a trauma, or after repeated instances in which people that are supposed to be there for us, are not. When someone consistently violates that trust, or mistreats us, it can throw a person into emotional turmoil, and false sense of identity, and we become

"Victims". Again, I am in no way downplaying the severity of the mistrust and abuse you may have experienced, just trying to lead you to a better way of thinking. Often when we have a victim mentality, we shirk our own responsibilities and blame absolutely everything on other people. We eventually learn to take zero responsibilities for our own actions, and spend all our time blaming others and feeling sorry for ourselves.

The next things you're probably going to ask, which I will help try to answer is 1) How do I know if I have victim mentality and 2) How do I change? Number one is easy to answer. If you answer "yes" to any of the next ten statements, there is a good chance that you suffer from a victim mentality. Answer these questions honestly, as it is only for you to know, and you to want to do something about.

- You truly think life is against you
- You always think that the worst thing that can happen will
- You take it personally and feel under attack when people try to give you helpful suggestions
- You blame everybody else when something goes wrong, even if you were the cause
- You tend to be attracted to people that complain a lot or think that life is bad and hard
- You feel like you have no control over circumstances in your life
- You find yourself getting angry with family and friends and you find yourself using the phrase "No one understands what I'm going through" a lot
- You find yourself putting yourself down a lot

114

- You spend a lot of time feeling sorry for yourself
- You do not believe that good things happening to you are possible
- You tend to hold grudges with people for things that happened a log time ago, and you hold onto that bitterness

- You lack self-confidence

There are more examples that I could use, but these are just a few. Do any of these sound familiar to you? If so, do you want to learn a few tricks to help you change your mind set? Yes? Read on. Remember, though, that this mindset was not made over night and it will take a little time, and a conscious effort to change.

- Validate your feelings - Accept that someone or something hurt your feelings, and then bury those feelings and move on
- Learn to forgive. When someone wrongs you, work to get on with it.
- Practice gratitude. Feel grateful for the things you have and spend less time focusing on what you don't have
- Take responsibility in the things you can control and learn to accept that responsibility instead of always looking for someone to blame. When you take responsibility, you will realize that you have the power to control future outcomes
- Take responsibility of your thoughts and replay the narrative with a different ending, doing your part to make it a better situation.
- Try to find the good in every situation. Victimization thrives on negativity and if you look for the good in a situation, the bad will seem less obvious

- Celebrate your small wins- this starts to build a little self-confidence and faith in yourself
- Challenge your limiting beliefs Start to really challenge things you never thought you could do, and believe you can when you start
- Think positive – remember, what you think about, you bring about.

We all have good days, bad days and days in between. Your goal to a happier you is to push through and make them as good as possible. Blaming others never fixed anything. If you want to experience more good in your life, you need to make a conscious decision to be that change toward the positive. Own up to what you've done, and know that you are going to make mistakes along the way. Nobody is perfect. Nobody is expecting you to be. But doing your best and creating the best NOW that you can is certainly better than sitting around complaining about what could have been , or waiting for the bad to come. Remember the verse "I can achieve all things through Christ who strengthen me", Phillipians 4:13? So get started today and make a better tomorrow, pushing through like the victor you were meant to be.

WISDOM

"GOD GRANT ME THE SERENITY TO ACCEPT THE
THINGS I CAN NOT CHANGE, THE COURAGE TO
CHANGE THE THINGS I CAN AND THE **WISDOM**
TO KNOW THE DIFFERENCE"

I know you are probably thinking to yourself that I already put that in the book. Great catch. However, I wanted to add it again for a few reasons. The first reason is that it is probably one of the verses that I repeated to myself the most during my beginning healing and two, I want to focus on the word "WISDOM" for this section alone.

What exactly is wisdom and where do we get it? Wikipedia defines wisdom as "The ability to contemplate and act using knowledge, experience, understanding, common sense and insight."[ix] That seems pretty all encompassing, doesn't it? Simple! We take what we know and what we have learned, and we apply it. Could it really be that simple? In a way, it is. However, it is also a very complex idea, one that many will argue, is not scientific, but philosophical in nature. Some will argue that only God can give us true wisdom.

To me, wisdom is a combination of all of these things. When I need to emerge more victorious from a situation, I do turn to

God for my understanding. In my mind, truth and wisdom come directly from His word. However, right now we are trying to discover for you, where to obtain this wisdom. In going through this book, I have thrown a lot of information at you. Some you may have already known, some may have been brand new information. Some may even have been things that you've heard before, but refuse to buy into. That is ok. That is what wisdom is. It is taking what you are presented with, applying it to your experiences and perception of a situation, and then ultimately, using the common sense, insight and understanding, giving yourself the authority to "know" the answer.

When you started reading this book, you may have been filled with questions. Were any of them answered? Does "stuff" make a little more sense now? Do you see how things that you thought were normal were not, and have you changed the way you look at anything? If so, you have gained wisdom! Congratulations. Now, I encourage you to seek more. As I mentioned in the beginning, this is a life-long journey of healing and recovery. With that comes wisdom beyond your wildest dreams. So how do you acquire more wisdom? Simple, expose yourself to new information as much as possible. Some things that I would suggest if you want to gain more wisdom.

1. Read more – there is a wealth of information at our fingertips
2. Talk to people that you have never met before. Meeting new people gives us a new perspective on topics we thought we knew about
3. Be open-minded- When you hear something new, process it completely before dismissing it. You may begin to look at it differently the more information that you have

4. Read the Book of Proverbs in the Bible. Soloman could have asked God for anything in the world, and he asked Him for Wisdom. His writings are filled with incredible examples of Gods words of wisdom. (Proverbs 9 is a good place to start)
5. Have a good mentor – This could be a teacher, pastor, or someone who you notice reacts to stressful situations calmly, thinking through things instead of flying off the handle
6. Use your pain and suffering to gain wisdom. With every painful experience, find out what you have learned from it
7. Admit you know little. Socrates said once that "The only true wisdom is in knowing you know nothing." Being humble in this aspect opens up the willingness to learn.
8. Work on improving your mental and emotional well being. When we are more grounded and in a better place mentally, we are more open to accepting information with a positive eye
9. Learn from making mistakes and know that it is ok not to be perfect. When we make mistakes, we learn from them.
10. Challenge your brain. Do things the hard way, instead of taking the easy way out. A good example of this is turning off your GPS in your car and having to figure out how to get there using your senses. Wakening all of your senses shows us how much more there is to experience in the world, and makes you see things in a different light.

I encourage you…. NO, I challenge you. Learn five new things a day and after awhile watch how the information just starts flooding in. Our minds yearn to be taught. We just need to encourage the learning. The more knowledge, the more you can apply it, and the more wise you will become.

EXAMINE (XRAY)

I am assuming while I write this, that this will be the toughest part of the book for some people. I know it would have been for me as a child. I definitely fell into the victim personality type as a teenager. Everything that happened to me was someone else's fault and there was nothing I could have done to do anything about any of it. I reacted and acted the way I did because of what was done to me, and I felt completely and totally justified to do so. After all, how could I be expected to be any different? I had been abused, locked in closets, beaten, had my shin broken with an iron, raped by my mothers drug dealers, pimped out to others. So why would I be expected to be a normal teen with a normal, well adjusted life? I shouldn't be, right? Absolutely WRONG! Some of the things I did back then I did not out of necessity, or survival. Some of them I did out of anger, out of spite, out of a complete and total disregard for my own self-respect or that of others. And now I know that . I didn't back then, though. That is for sure.

Right now you are still probably at the anger state. You are angry that life is treating you the way it is, and that you are having to go through the things you are going through. However, is it changing how you act to others? Is it making you the kind of person that not only do you not like, but that you would never want to be? This is the part where you have to really take a look at yourself and see what you have become. Our actions that we can control are our own choices, and they need to come from the right place. I am asking you to examine yourself, not so that you can find faults, but so that you can truly see where your actions and thoughts are coming from. I am asking you to do this because you can't truly heal until you know and love who you truly are.

If you go back to the section on Higher Power, you will remember that I listed the 12 steps of recovery for the Alanon and Alateen program. Reread steps four through ten. If you notice they are all about you. When I was a teen and I read that , I was so confused. What could I have possibly done? I was the one being wronged. I was soooo wrong. I had hurt people. I had lied and stolen, and been mean to people that were only trying to help me. I had treated my High School boyfriend terribly, and been unnecessarily mean to others that didn't deserve it. I guess I was going through a period of entitlement. I thought that if I had emerged victoriously out of something so dark, the world owed me, on my terms. I regret those things now, and have made amends to the people that I could.

All I am asking of you is that you really examine who you are. Who you truly are. Are you the person that you want to be? We all need work in my humble opinion. I am not saying you have flaws (although none of us are perfect). I am simply saying that many of us are in a dark place for so long that we forget some of the basic skills necessary to have a happy life. Some of the traits I forgot I had in me were love, compassion, empathy, understanding and a feeling of gratitude. I worked very hard through the years to get those back and now I know when I am veering from who I want to be. When you know, and acknowledge it in yourself, it is much easier to work to make the change. That is really all I am saying.

K.F., Alanon member said: "No one told me the burden I would release by accepting my own behavior as a cause of my misery. I felt like a victim and as long as I blamed others that meant I had no power to change and grow. My 4th Step has allowed me to truly let go. I let go of the shame and guilt. I released myself from the prison of my own self- hatred. I can't yet say I love myself - but I am now able to treat myself with kindness and forgiveness."

I myself, do Step 4 every year. I think that God never reveals things to me about myself that I am not ready to handle. He gives it to me at the perfect time. I will continue with my personal inventory over and over again, each time finding more and more about myself that I can be proud of, and things I can work on. I encourage you to do the same.

YOU

So we are almost at the end, and by now I am hoping and praying that you have realized the common theme of the book. It is that YOU are the most important part of this whole equation. Horrible things are going on around you. There is abuse, neglect, trauma and a number of other atrocities that you are having to witness, endure and survive. Surviving will only be possible if you take care of yourself. My grandma used to play this little song for me called "The most important person". I urge you to look it up on You Tube. Just type in "The Most Important Person In the World". It still makes me smile and think of her every time I listen to it. The gist of it is "The most important person in the whole wide world is you!" I don't know how to say it any differently. It is vital at this stage that if you want to recover and start to heal some of your wounds that you have sustained, that you begin RIGHT NOW to nourish your well being. That means your physical well being, your mental well being and most importantly , your spiritual well being. By now you have heard me stress it over and over, and I am not going to beat a dead horse by repeating it again…. No, that's not true.. One more time, just so you get it. It is time RIGHT NOW, to start to take good care of yourself. It won't be instantly. It will take time, and love and patience with yourself. You've spent your life becoming who you are based on the only tactics and coping skills that you had at the time. You've developed strategies to survive, and I commend you. Now it's time to take what you've learned and start to not just survive, but THRIVE!

On another note, and a point that I waited until very far into the book to mention, let's really talk about you…..

How are you really doing? What are you feeling? How bad are the thoughts that run through your head at night when you go to sleep? Are there nightmares? Day terrors? Triggers that make you want to run away screaming? Anxiety that you can't get to settle down? Massive depression that makes you want to harm yourself? Are you starting to self-soothe by using drugs or alcohol? Are you doing things that you know are not right, but you can't seem to stop?

If so, all of this is normal and honestly, somewhat to be expected. If you are feeling things to this extent, however, I think it is safe to say that you may need professional help. Please go seek out someone that can talk to you on a professional level, and diagnose what is really going on with you. While many of the things you are experiencing may come from the traumatic events of your life, there may also be underlying causes. Talking to a health professional can help you find that out. And I urge you not to wait.

I mentioned in the beginning that there is no one cause for alcoholism that they can trace. I also mentioned that just because your parent is an alcoholic does not mean you are too. However, there are mental health issues, which are very controllable, that bring upon some of the traits that may have made your parent start drinking to begin with. It is somewhat of a "Which came first, the chicken or the egg" question. Did your parent start drinking because of something terrible that happened to them, or was there an underlying mental health issue that caused the drinking? Do they drink to heal that pain, or is that pain because they drink? Those questions may be ones that you need to find out the answer for your own situation. You owe it to yourself. All the happy thoughts and practice in the world won't help 100% if there is a physiological reason for what you are feeling, and it is not just the trauma that brought it about. Visit the list of resources, if you feel that the time is right, and let a professional get you to the place you need to be. But be honest with yourself.

Remember, there is no shame in any of this. It is a rough world that we live in, and you have experienced and dealt with more than the average person can even begin to imagine. You absolutely owe it to yourself, 100%, to be able to heal and thrive, and take this world by storm.

ZEN

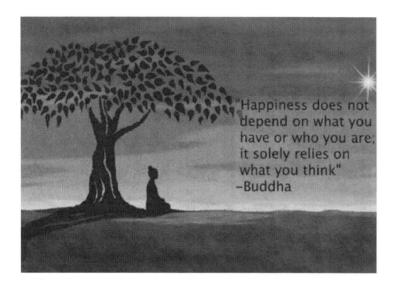

"Happiness does not depend on what you have or who you are; it solely relies on what you think"
–Buddha

What do you think of when you hear people talking about Zen? Is it a Buddhist monk sitting on the ground with a brown robe and bare feet? Then you are right there with a lot of people, and not too far off. Why is it the stereotype? Because they do sit a lot! They sit and they feel and they exist in the presence. Zen is "A Japanese School of Mahayana Buddhism emphasizing the value of meditation and intuition."ˣ (Collins English Dictionary. Glasgow: HarperCollins Publishers, 1994. Print) For our purposes, however, we are going to look at the word "Zen" as more of a lifestyle. An adjective. A way of describing a life of internal peace and contentment, free of judgement and hatred towards any other human being. Simply put, BLISS!

Zen, the Zen we want to achieve is "A state of calm attentiveness in which one's actions are guided by intuition rather than a conscious effort." (Merriam Webster Dictionary) This is the one that we are shooting for. So what does it mean to you, and your search for peace and tranquility? It means a different way of looking at things. It means being present in the moment and focusing on your inner self. It means being at a state of peace with your place in the universe , and your own thoughts. While it is hard to put an exact definition to it, it is important to understand how implementing some of its basic core principles can have a huge impact on your days, every day.

What exactly are the basic ideas behind a zen lifestyle? This is such a simple explanation to a very complex and intricate religion/philosophy, of which it is honestly, neither. For now I simply want to do a quick introduction. I encourage you to Google information about a zen lifestyle and practice some of the ideas that you read about. The whole idea behind a zen lifestyle is that you are trying to awaken your inner self, including your compassion and wisdom. You look at yourself without judgement or condemnation, and understand that things "Just Are". These periods of enlightenment, are most likely reached during practices of meditation and silence, where external thoughts and beliefs are not permitted to enter, thereby silencing the distractions of all the external "Noise" that exists in our busy lives.

So, how do we reach this state of happiness, we call Zen? How do we live a Zen lifestyle? If you ask someone that has truly committed his/her life to this lifestyle, it will involve a whole lot of discipline, practice, and absolute commitment. If you want to get started in the right direction, however, it is never to early to start. You may find that practicing some of these simple techniques may calm you in such a way that you start to desire more and more of it. It certainly did for me. ...

10 Tips to Living a More "Zen" Lifestyle

TIP #1. Wake up early - starting the day rushing, late and frazzled is a terrible start to a calm day. Wake early and allow yourself time to get where you're going

TIP #2. - Tidy up your environment- Living among clutter keeps you from enjoying the here and now. If you are always looking around at a mess, your mind wanders and keeps you from focusing on the "Nothingness" and peacefulness of just being

TIP #3- Do one thing at a time, and focus on that one thing- When you are eating, enjoy the taste of the food, and the act of eating. When you are bathing, enjoy the shower and think about the warm water and peacefulness. When you are walking, just enjoy the sights that you see RIGHT NOW. Doing two things at once takes away the simplicity of one enjoyable act.

TIP #4- Finish what you start- When you start something, finish it. Moving from one task to another and never finishing anything leaves you devoid of a sense of accomplishment, and always stressed about a "TO DO LIST" that never gets smaller.

TIP #5- Schedule what you have to do, and do only those things. Try to eliminate the things in your life that are not productive or necessary. You will find that you have more time for the things that you enjoy and that contribute to your overall happiness

TIP #6- Smile Often- Did you know that when you smile a genuine smile, it is impossible for you to be thinking negative thoughts? That is just how the brain works. Smiling often, especially around other people is contagious. You will soon notice that there are more things to smile about, and more people willing to share those happy moments with you

TIP #7- Eat healthy food- Eating healthy food that truly nourishes our bodies is a great way to start each day. You will feel better for it, and your energy levels will be increased. If you do not have regular access to healthy foods, talk to someone that can help you gain access to them. You will not be sorry.

TIP #8- Exercise often - Just as eating healthy is great for you, so is exercise. This does not have to be a mile run, or high intensity workouts. Just stretching and moving around, or dancing by yourself in a room is enough to get the blood pumping. Exercise has been shown to increase levels of dopamine, the natural feel good hormone, and when our dopamine is higher, you are less likely to suffer from bouts of stress and anxiety. So get out there and move!

TIP #9 - Leave time in your schedule between activities. Scheduling too much into one day can leave you feeling rushed, stressed and worried. Schedule time between each activity. That will leave you time to just sit and enjoy the time, or even just time to sit and do NOTHING! Which leads me to the most important tip/ trick for achieving a zen lifestyle...

TIP #10- Meditate regularly. Students of the zen lifestyle always have time in their day to just sit and do nothing. You can literally do this anywhere, although outside in nature is thought to be the most peaceful. The Chinese call this Zazen, and it literally just means sitting meditation. It is considered to be the most important part of the day for anyone living by the Zen principles. It means being oneself, with nothing extra, in harmony with the way things are. It is the simple practice of looking directly at things the way they are, and should be practiced as often as possible.[xi]

Does that help at all? Do you think that you could practice throwing even just a few of these tricks into your daily routine? I urge you to try and see what a difference it can make.

FINAL THOUGHTS

From A to Z, and everywhere in between, there is something to learn about being the child of an alcoholic. I sincerely hope that you have learned some valuable information, and you can use that information to continue on in your healing journey. I wish nothing but the best for you. Practice what you learned, use your new tools you were given, and never stop believing in yourself.

I want to end by saying that if you get one thing out of this entire book, I want it to be this.....

You Have One Job! One! That is to take care of you. You read this book for a reason. You want to fix everything around you. You want to control all circumstances and outcomes. That is not your job. Let me repeat myself..... YOU HAVE ONE JOB! Your job is to do whatever you have to do to become a happier, healthier, safer YOU! That is how you are going to THRIVE and come out of this a victor. I know you can do it. I have faith in you. Have faith in yourself.

I hope you have enjoyed the book. If so, please kindly leave a review on Amazon. I appreciate you sharing the word with those that need it.

ENDNOTES

1. Branden, Nathaniel. The Six Pillars of Self-Esteem. Nathaniel Brandon Audio Renaissance, 1994.

2. https://childwelfare.gov Child Welfare Information Gateway. 2020.

3. https://www.niaaa.nih.gov.brochures-and-fact-sheets. Alcohol- Induced Blackouts. 2018

4. Al-Anon's Twelve Steps, copyright 1996 by Al-Anon Family Group.

5. Piper, John Desiring God Foundation (https://www.desiringgod.org)

6. Tony A, 1978. The Laundry List- 14 Traits of an Adult Child of An Alcoholic. https;//adultchildren.org

7. Collins English Dictionary. Glasgow: HarperCollins Publishers, 1994. Print

8. What is Zazen? Zoto Zen Buddhist Association. https://www.szba.org/what-is-zazen

9. Wisdom in Wikipedia. (ND) https://en.wikipedia.org/wisdom

Made in the USA
Columbia, SC
16 February 2023

12495092R00080